COLLECTOR'S GUIDE TO

Letter

Openers

IDENTIFICATION & VALUES

EVERETT
GRIST

COLLECTOR BOOKS
A Division of Schroeder Publishing Co., Inc.

The current values in this book should be used only as a guide. They are not intended to set prices, which vary from one section of the country to another. Auction prices as well as dealer prices vary greatly and are affected by condition as well as demand. Neither the Author nor the Publisher assumes responsibility for any losses that might be incurred as a result of consulting this guide.

Searching For A Publisher?

We are always looking for knowledgeable people considered to be experts within their fields. If you feel that there is a real need for a book on your collectible subject and have a large comprehensive collection, contact Collector Books.

Cover design: Beth Summers
Book design: Joyce Cherry

Contents

Foreword

By Kevin and Marilyn Kenne

The letter opener is, for the most part, a tool used to open envelopes swiftly and neatly without damaging the contents. To understand the need for such a tool, we must first briefly discuss the history of written messages.

As early as 485 B.C., the Greek traveler Herodotus writes, "Neither snow, nor rain, nor gloom of night stays these couriers from the swift completion of their appointed rounds." Prison or execution awaited those Greek couriers who were lax or incompetent in their duties. Too bad such an incentive to excel at your job doesn't apply today.

The first postal systems were used by governments to transport written information and to communicate with remote areas of their kingdoms. They were used to send orders and proclaim new laws, as well as keep track of taxes or tributes paid. Most of these early messages traveled in sealed pouches. The Greeks and Romans had a sophisticated postal system, and such famous rulers as Genghis Khan (1162 – 1227), Charlemagne, and King Henry the VIII established such services.

By the fifteenth century, the House of Thurn and Taxis had developed a postal system in Europe. At first, they served only the royal princes of Europe, but in 1505 they opened this system to the paying public. They continued in Europe until approximately 1872. By then, the governments of most civilized countries of the world had set up their own systems.

Whereas governmental messages traveled in sealed pouches, private mail was open to prying eyes. Some time in the early eighteenth century, people felt such a strong need for privacy that they began folding the message and then folding another piece of paper around it, upon which they wrote the address. These early envelopes were then sealed with wax and impressed with a seal. In order to open these letters without damaging the contents, a pocket knife or "letter opener" was used.

Early letter openers might have been almost any sharp blade small enough to do the job. As the volume of mail increased, a constantly used knife became something with which to cut one's hand. In these early days, even minor cuts that became infected could easily prove fatal eventually, as no antibiotics existed. So, gradually a duller instrument was developed. These new letter openers also developed into highly crafted tools. The rich favored ivory, mother of pearl, and silver. The rest of humanity used less exotic materials such as wood, steel, brass, and horn. By the late nineteenth century, the letter opener had become a popular advertising give-away item. Many were made of metal and celluloid with plain or figural handles. As letter openers became mass produced, many took on dual roles. They served not only to open letters, but also as a magnifier, ruler, pen or pencil, can opener, paperweight, calendar, paper creaser, etc. Mass production also gave rise to letter openers as souvenirs. Some of the more desirable ones had stanhopes inset in their handles.

Today, letter openers can be found made of almost any material, shape, and style. The products and places advertised on them are too numerous to mention. Figural shapes are very collectible as are the gadget ones. The most common shapes are knife and sword like. Interesting or crossover advertising pieces are also in demand. Rare, expensive, or exotic materials also affect prices. The most common are some of the souvenir pieces and insurance company advertisements.

In the late nineteenth century through the early twentieth century, letter openers were also called "letter knives." A large number of these were produced in sterling, silver plate, agate, ivory, tortoise, jade, and mother of pearl for the genteel members of society. The blades were generally of silver, silver plate, mother of pearl, or ivory and sterling combinations. The most desirable from this period are those novelty "letter knives" which are cast figures of owls, dogs, foxes, cats, or sporting motifs.

Introduction

The question is: If it isn't listed in any encyclopedia, Webster's Dictionary, or the Oxford English Dictionary, does it really exist? Maybe it is just a figment of our imagination! The OED is supposedly the epitome of research tools, listing even old, outdated tools with a clear, concise definition. How else would we know today what a flax brake was or what it did? Or a pot trammel?

However, after much searching through various encyclopedias — Colliers, World Book, etc., (Funk and Wagnalls briefly lists it under postal history) — and various dictionaries, including the OED, I find that the word(s) letteropener/letter opener are virtually unlisted. Does this mean these objects do not exist? Of course not, but they seem to have lacked the appeal necessary for the editors to include a listing for these items. Even under the topic "envelope," only a little more is printed in stamp and postal collectible books. Only brief attention is paid by the authors/editors of art-related books. It seems, therefore, that we are breaking new ground here.

I have surmised that letter openers are called such because they were once used to open letters, not envelopes, the envelope being a relatively modern invention. In medieval days when only the elite could read or write, the elite being the monarch, titled personages, and clergy, epistles relaying ideas or information were written on a sheet of very expensive parchment (production costs were high, you know). The letter was then folded over, such as we now fold letters to put them into envelopes, and the overlapping part was sealed with sealing wax, into which a personal seal was stamped before the wax hardened. In the case of the monarch, the state seal was used. An example of one of these wax seal breakers is included in the photos.

As with most collectible items, letter openers have been produced in probably every solid medium available, except maybe paper. One of the oldest letter openers described as such was produced circa 100-1 BCE, during the Western Han dynasty in China. It would surprise no one to learn that China, who also has one of the oldest postal systems, was one of the first to produce letter openers. Mail being reserved for royalty, their letter openers were often made of jade. Chinese archeology only came under government control in the 1920s, thus the archeologists opportunity to see the artifacts in the grave was, more often than not, lost, and their expertise disengaged before they had a chance to start their examination. So the precise dating of early Chinese letter openers is, at best, an educated guess.

Believe it or not, jade (jadeite and nephrite) is a white or colorless stone. The great range of colors in which it is found — green, brown, mauve, blue, yellow, red, gray, and black — is due to the presence of minute quantities of other elements such as iron, chromium, or manganese.

Other media used in the production of early letter openers are of animal origin — ivory, bone, horn, and shell. These materials were among man's earliest art material. When naturally occurring acids are absent, and ivory, shell, or bone objects are not destroyed by fire, we find they are nearly imperishable. Not only do these materials provide a permanent record, they are materials which have been in constant use worldwide, throughout the ages. All are still being used today by craftsmen, artists, and jewelers. Horn artifacts are attacked by insects and often show worm or burrow damage.

Instead of being the end product, horn was relegated to the status of tool when the use of metals evolved. Horn is a plastic material after it is boiled. It is that quality which made it useful in a variety of ways where plasticity was important, such as in the making of spoons, buttons, and in fashioning containers for gunpowder.

The second animal by-product, bone, was easily cleaned and was grease repellent, which made it highly suitable for the making of spoons, gunpowder containers, combs, and knitting needles.

Ivory, such as that from the elephant and walrus, was another material used over the years. So, too, were animal tusks, such as that of the wild boar. Both new ivory and fossilized ivory have been used for decorative objects, the fossilized being much darker than the new material. The older the item in question, the more decorative it tends to be. It is as if, in this day of instant gratification, it takes too much time to produce a nicely fashioned item or a highly decorative object for everyday use. Also, the price would probably be prohibitive in today's high labor cost market.

From the onset of the use of letter openers during the first part of the eighteenth century, its use "exploded," and letter openers became a generally owned and used item by 1860. I would suggest that the increased popularity of the item could be correlated to the increased levels of education and the greater affordability of mail services to the average consumer. As the new information super highway and e-mail increase, the letter opener may some day be relegated to be obsolete.

As noted earlier, today's letter openers are produced in almost every solid material; however, those of quality workmanship and design are made of the more desirable materials. Many of the media used in production are shown in the photos contained herein. Openers were made of malachite, jasper, tiger eye, and jade from the semi-precious stone medium. Sterling silver was a more suitable medium than gold because of the softness of gold in its purer states; brass, stainless steel, and pot metal were also used. Man-made substances include Delft (pottery), French ivory (celluloid), and glass. Not to forget Mother Nature, openers are also fashioned of wood.

Letter openers have often done double duty, such as having a magnifying glass on the handle, a ball point pen, a ruler, or a cigarette lighter. They are decorated with animals, clowns, Amish couples, windmills, advertisements, and subjects too numerous to mention. They are fashioned after scimitars, sabers, hunting knives, bayonets, and daggers. There is virtually a letter opener aimed at the collecting desires of almost anyone, from quilters to Dutch-ophiles, from weapons collectors to advertising collectors, from aluminum buffs to sterling silver aficionados. The opener portion of the item may be fashioned to resemble the tail of a pheasant, a lady's leg, a marlin's bill, a lizard's tail, a fish tail, or an elf's hat.

We hope you enjoy the plates provided in this book. The variety and workmanship can keep you interested for hours on end, just examining the intricacy of the design and attention to detail. The price of letter openers as a collectible is within the reach of most people. Many fine examples can be found for under $10.00, although the sky is the limit for those made of better materials and/or with highly sought quality artistic design.

Happy collecting!

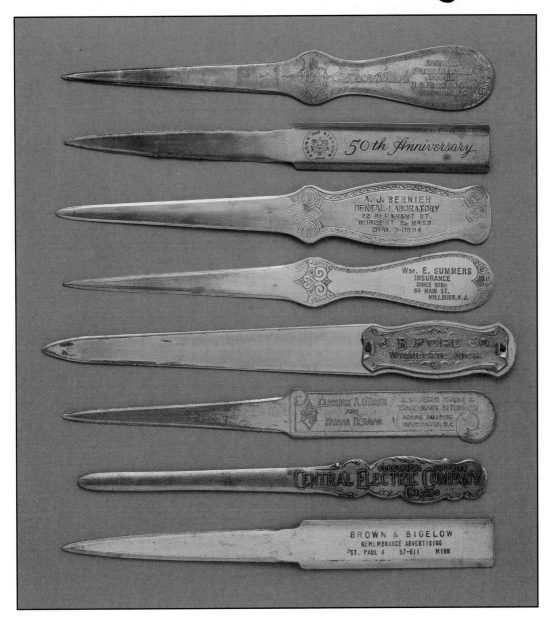

Plate 1. Top to bottom.

METAL — BRASS

Clarence A. O'Brien, Patent Attorney $35.00
Brown & Bigelow, 1896–1946, 50th Anniversary $35.00
A. J. Bernier — Dental Laboratory $25.00
Wm. E. Summers Ins., Since 1886 . . . .$25.00
J. B. Ford Co. $40.00
Clarence A. O'Brien and Hyman Berman $35.00
Central Electric Co. of Chicago, OKONITE $45.00
Brown & Bigelow — Remembrance Advertising $30.00

Plate 2. Left to right.

METAL — BRASS UNLESS OTHERWISE STATED

Diversified Industries, Inc., Roseville, Mich, stamped B & B, St. Paul Minn. $22.00
Bronze, Ernst Kaufmann, Inc., Spruce St., N.Y. $22.00
Clarence A. O'Brien, Registered Patent Attorney $35.00
Clarence A. O'Brien, Registered Patent Attorney $35.00
Life & Casualty Ins. Co. of Tenn., Nashville, Tune in on WLAC $25.00
Clarence A. O'Brien, Registered Patent Attorney (on reverse side are his instructions
    for applying for patents) $35.00
Stamped Genuine Bronze, W&H Co., Newark, N. J., The Whitehead & Hoag Co., We Excel in
    Bronze $45.00
Bronze, The Robbins & Myers Co., Springfield, Oh $35.00
Stamped Genuine Bronze, W&H Co., Newark, N. J., Grandin's Stock Food, Jamestown, N.Y.,
    red enameled shield $40.00

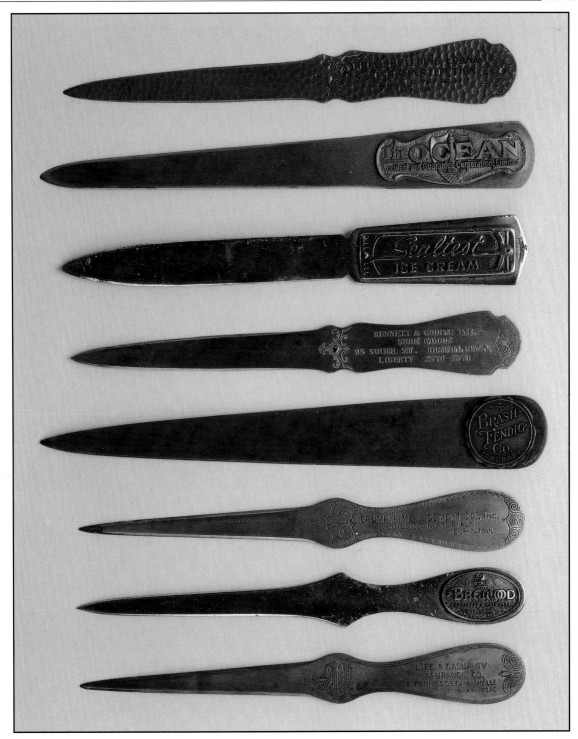

Plate 3. Top to bottom.

METAL

Bronze, made by Metal Arts Co., Serial Building Loan & Savings Institution, Organized 1885 .$35.00
Brass, The Ocean Accident and Guarantee Corporation $25.00
Stamped Genuine Bronze, made by W&H Co., Newark, N.J., Sealtest Ice Cream, double sided $40.00
Bronze, made by the Metal Arts Co., Bennett & Goding, Inc., Shoe Goods $25.00
Genuine Bronze, made by The Metal Arts Co., Brash-Fendig Co., Insurers $35.00
Brass, Crump Lime & Cement Co., Inc., Building Materials, Memphis, Tenn. $35.00
Bashan Bros. Co., Rochester, N.Y., Brewood Engravers & Printers $25.00
Brass, Life & Casualty Ins. Co., Nashville, Tenn. $25.00

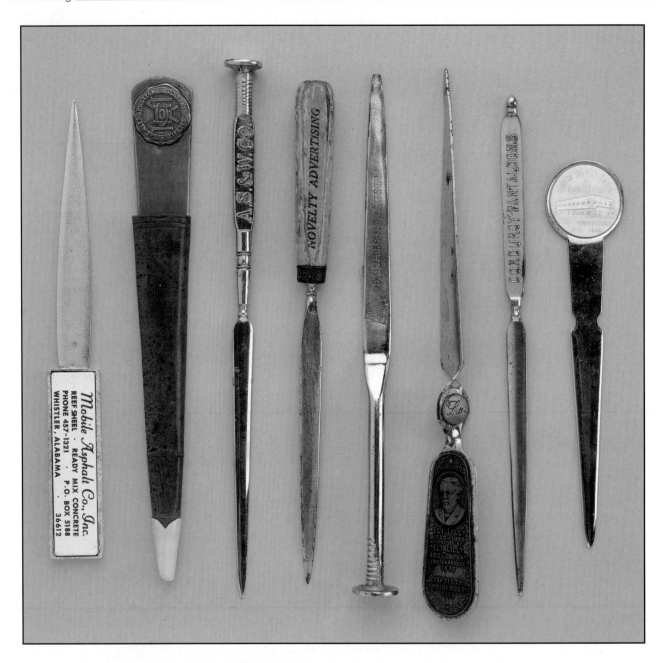

Plate 4. Left to right.

METAL

White metal, Mobile Asphalt Co., Inc., Whistler, Ala. $6.00
Bronze, in leather sheath with celluloid tip, The Metropolitan Life Ins. Co. $35.00
Chrome steel, A. S. & W. Co. $12.00
Wood and steel, Novelty Advertising, C. E. Wildman, Thomasville, Ga. $20.00
Steel, Pittsburgh Steel Co., also stamped on nail head, Pittsburgh Steel $18.00
Chrome steel and bronze, Eli Lilly, 1838–1898, Founder Eli Lilly and Company, Fiftieth
    Anniversary 1926 (on guard, oval bronze plaque, stamped Lilly) $25.00
Steel, L. I. Meyer & Co., Montoursville, Pa. $12.00
Steel, First State Bank of Monticello $6.00

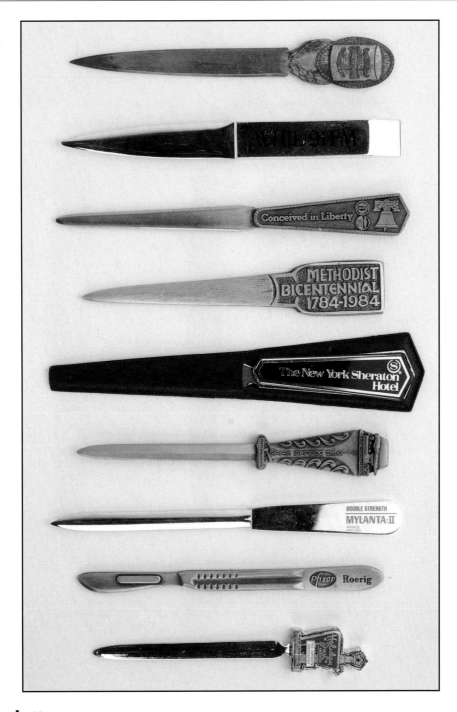

Plate 5. Top to bottom.

METAL

Bronze, stamped Metal Arts Co., Rochester, N.Y., The W. N. Clark Co., Canned Foods,
    Rochester, N. Y. $25.00
Brass, WHIL-91FM $8.00
Pewter, Conceived in Liberty, Ed Godwin's Personnel© Service, Inc. $8.00
Brass, Methodist Bicentennial, 1784–1984 . . . .$6.00
Plastic handle and brass with plastic sheath, New York, Sheraton Hotel $6.00
Pewter, R.M.D.C. Gish ©, Silver Dollar City $6.00
Brass, Double Strength Mylanta II $6.00
Cast white metal, three dimensional, Scapple, Pfizer, Roerig, reverse side, Unasyn $8.00
Gold plated, Holiday Inns of America $6.00

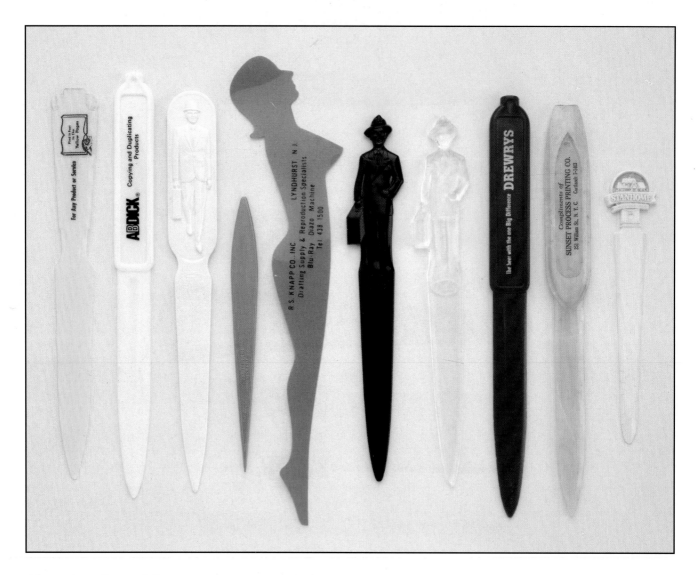

Plate 6. Left to right.

PLASTIC

Yellow Pages $3.00
A. B. Dick $3.00
Fuller Brush Man, reverse side is Fuller Brush Woman $12.00
Use this Letter Opener and see how you can save $3.00 . . . .$2.00
R. S. Knapp Co. Inc., shape of a woman $4.00
Fuller Brush Man (black) $6.00
Fuller Brush Man (clear) $4.00
Drewry's Beer $4.00
Sunset Process Printing Co., New York City $4.00
Stanhome $3.00

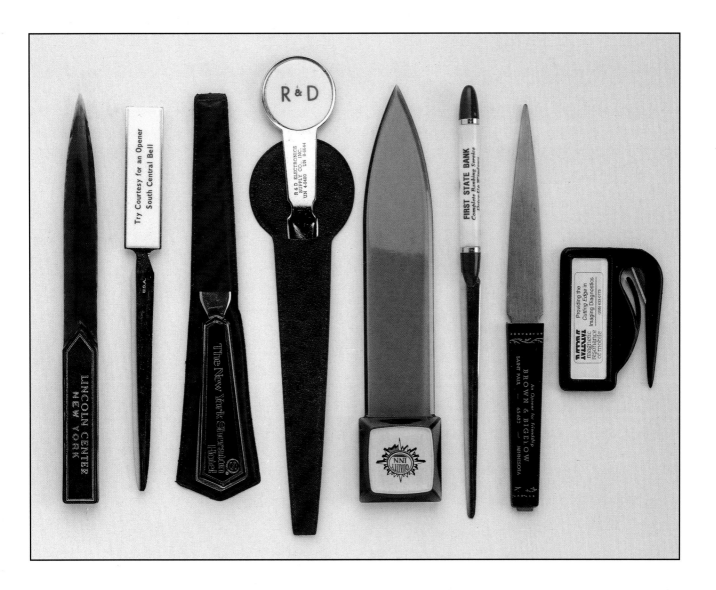

Plate 7. Left to right.

MISCELLANEOUS

Plastic, Lincoln Center, New York	$3.00
Plastic and steel, South Central Bell	$4.00
Plastic and steel, in plastic sheath, The New York Sheraton Hotel	$6.00
Plastic and steel, R & D Electronics	$4.00
Plastic, Quality Inn, Mobile Ala.	$4.00
Plastic and steel, First State Bank	$5.00
Bronze and plastic, stamped Brown & Bigelow, Remembrance®, St. Paul, Minn., Brown & Bigelow	$4.00
Magnetic Resonance of Mobile	$3.00

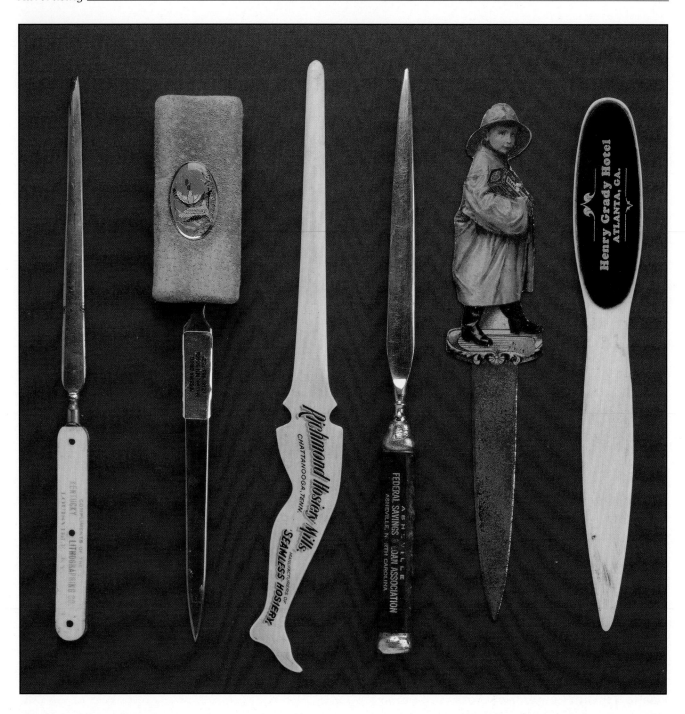

Plate 8. Left to right.

M<small>ISCELLANEOUS</small>

French ivory and steel, Kentucky Lithographing, Co., Louisville, KY $14.00
Leather, plastic, and brass with foil sticker, NISSWA Drug, NISSWA, MN $6.00
French ivory, Richmond Hosiery Mills, Chattanooga, TN $35.00
Leather and steel, Asheville Federal Savings & Loan Association $10.00
Lithographed metal, Uneeda Biscuits $50.00
Black celluloid and French ivory, Henry Grady Hotel, Atlanta, GA $30.00

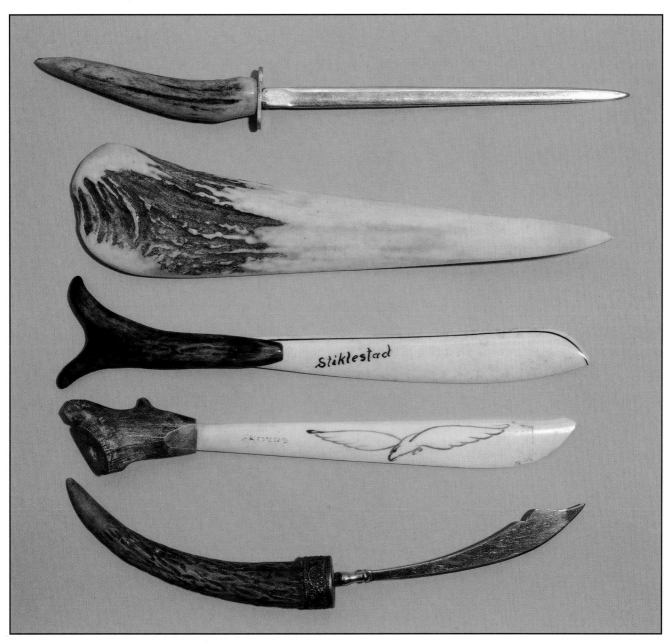

Plate 9. Top to bottom.

Stag and steel $10.00
Antler $35.00
Bone and faux antler, marked Stiklestad $10.00
Stag and bone, artist signed, Koras $15.00
Stag with sterling collar and steel, pat. Nov. 22, 1887 . . . .$25.00

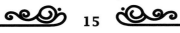

Plate 10. Left to right.

Stag and bone, marked Dovregubben $15.00
Antler and stainless steel, Nordic scene $15.00
Labeled Genuine Stag Horn, with leather sheath $12.00
Bone and faux stag $10.00
Stag with Montana on handle $8.00

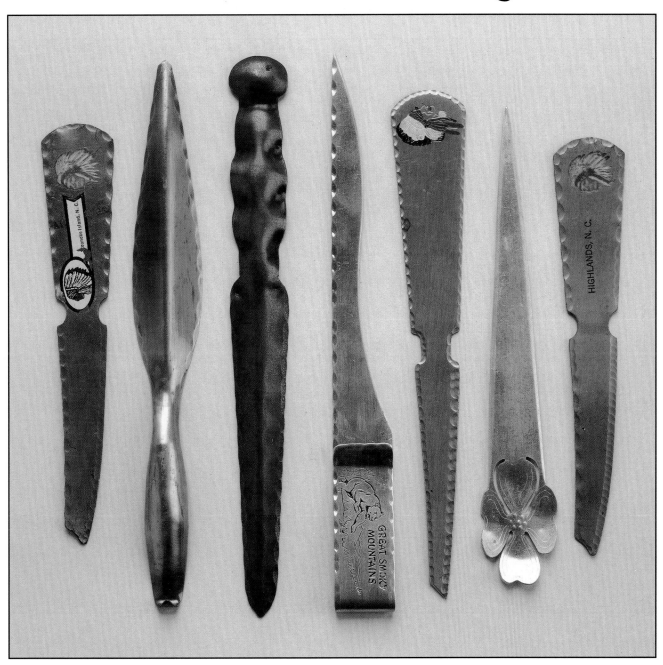

Plate 11. Left to right.

Copper, Roanoke Island, N. C. $10.00
Copper $10.00
Copper, stamped Vermont Hand Hammered Copper 705, Monogrammed CVC $12.00
Aluminum, Great Smoky Mountains, with letter holder as part of handle $12.00
Copper, painted war bonnet $8.00
Aluminum, cut out dogwood on handle $15.00
Copper, Highlands, N. C. $10.00

Plate 12. Left to right.

Cut-out totem $20.00
Carved decoration with paint $12.00
Paint with engraving work $10.00
Wood handle, decorated with dye and scrimshaw work, marked Mexico $15.00
Carved, marked Frogherseterur $10.00
Carved and pierced handle with painted scene, Souvenir of Mexico $15.00
Carved handle with painted woman $10.00
Purple wood handle with painted scene, Mexico $15.00
Carved totem with gold and black decal, printed on decal: Douglas Lodge, Itasca State Park .$18.00

Plate 13. Left to right.

Scrimshaw, marked LCKSAND $25.00
Carved and painted, Souvenir of Hugo, Okla. $20.00
Carved and pierced $35.00
Stenciled, marked Stalheim $15.00
Decal transfer, marked Rãttuik $15.00
Carved floral, ca. 1870, made for letters with wax seals $55.00
Carved and painted $10.00
Carved animal $15.00
Walrus bone, carved polar bear $45.00
Painted, marked Röros $12.00

Brass & Metals

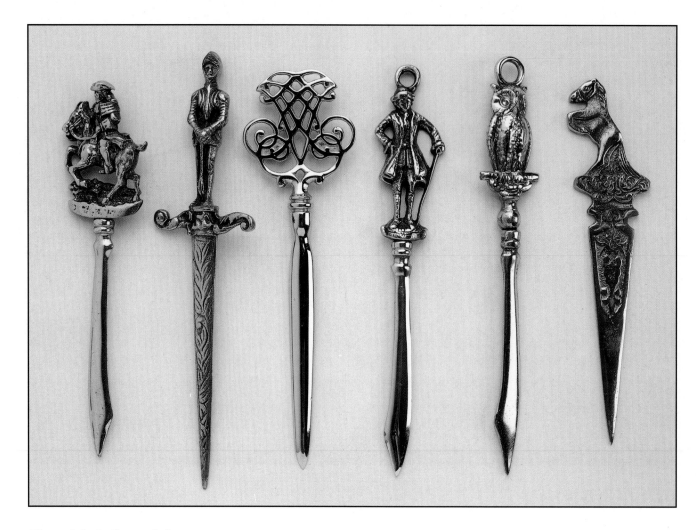

Plate 14. Left to right.

BRASS

Revolutionary patriot on horse, back marked England $10.00
Knight in armor, stamped England $10.00
Sand cast brass, by Virginia Metal Casters $15.00
American patriot, stamped England $10.00
Owl $10.00
Horse, rampant $10.00

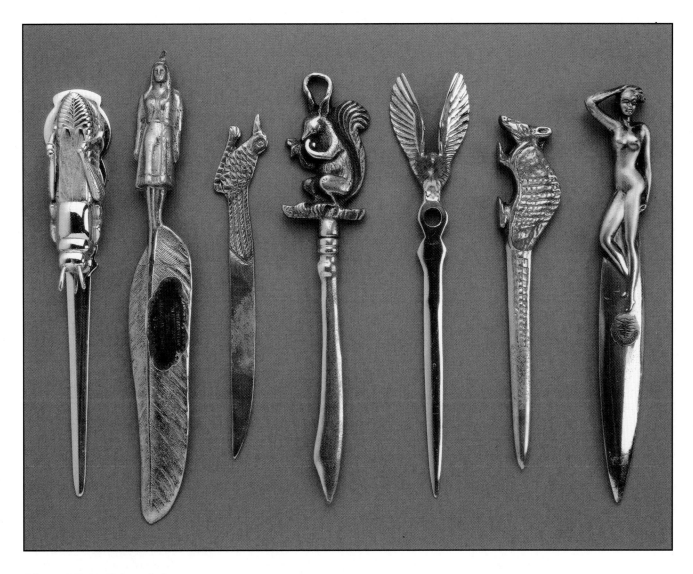

Plate 15. Left to right.

BRASS

3-D grasshopper, paperweight handle. $20.00
Pocahontas, back marked Pocahontas, Jamestown 1607 Virginia cr. 1957, Virginia Metal
    Workers $25.00
Bird $10.00
Squirrel, stamped England $12.00
Eagle $15.00
Armadillo $12.00
Nude woman 3-D, Great Smoky Mountains $18.00

Plate 16. Left to right.

BRASS

Bronze, rampant lion with scepter, royal seal $10.00
Minerva, back marked India $12.00
Griffin $10.00
Abstract $8.00
Lion with wings on pilar $10.00
Dragon's head with erotic scene on blade $35.00
Dragon $12.00

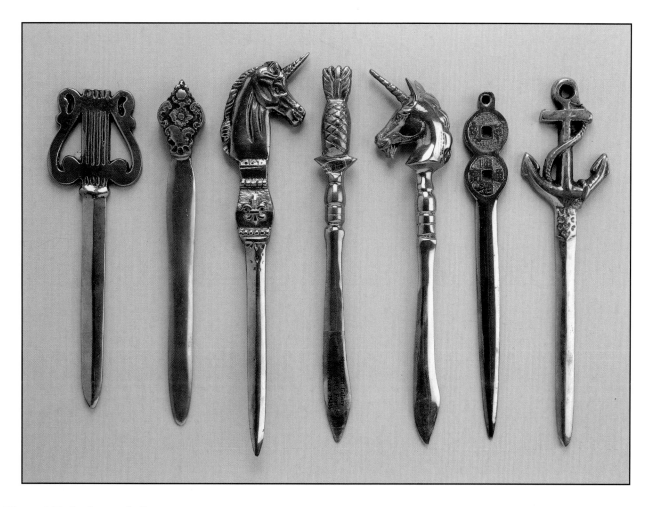

Plate 17. Left to right.

BRASS

Lyre, stamped Penco, New Bedford, Mass., made in Taiwan, ROC $10.00
Crest $6.00
Unicorn $12.00
Pineapple, made in Taiwan $8.00
Unicorn, made in Taiwan $10.00
Two Chinese coins $6.00
Anchor $8.00

Plate 18. Left to right.

BRASS

Scottie dog, marked England $15.00
Eagle, marked 7-46, Virginia Metal Crafters $20.00
Capt. John Smith, back marked Capt. John Smith, Jamestown — 1607 — Virginia, © 1957,
 Virginia Metal Crafters $25.00
Fox hunt, marked England $15.00
Roman soldier with shield, marked Italy $12.00

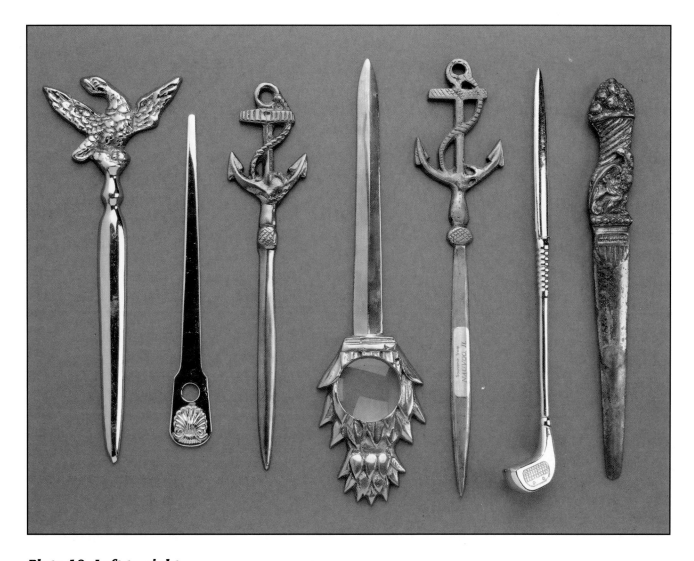

Plate 19. Left to right.

BRASS

Eagle, 7-47, Virginia Metal Crafters $20.00
Sea shell, stamped with anchor and P.M. at Flukes $8.00
Anchor, Souvenir of Nauvoo, Ill. $10.00
Magnifying pineapple top $10.00
Anchor $8.00
Gold-plated golf club $12.00
Eagle with cornucopia $15.00

Plate 20. Left to right.

BRASS

Compote with flowers $12.00
Upright rabbit $12.00
Elephant $10.00
Knight in armor $12.00
Satyr with pan pipes and bird $12.00
Rearing horse, England $12.00
Whale $12.00

Plate 21. Left to right.

Brass

Rooster $8.00
Falstaff, marked Peerage, England $15.00
Horse leg and hoof, England $10.00
Pineapple $8.00
Schooner with three masts $12.00
Imp, Lombard $12.00

Plate 22. Left to right.

BRASS

Oriental dragon with bottle opener top $12.00
A. Galleon 1558, Peerage, England $8.00
Stag $12.00
Cherub, Momento $12.00
Anchor $12.00
Cherub $12.00
Horse Shoe $8.00
Bear with Alaskan flag crest $10.00
Pisces, TERRASANG Creations, 1966 . . . .$8.00

Plate 23. Left to right.

BRASS

Bronze, by Benedict, white painted lady's head postage stamp $15.00
Sword, made in Hong Kong $6.00
Plain brass $4.00
Plain brass $6.00
Hammered handle $6.00
Branch and fruit motif $8.00
Twelve signs of the zodiac, back painted blue, Rafi $8.00
Chinese coins, Korea $6.00

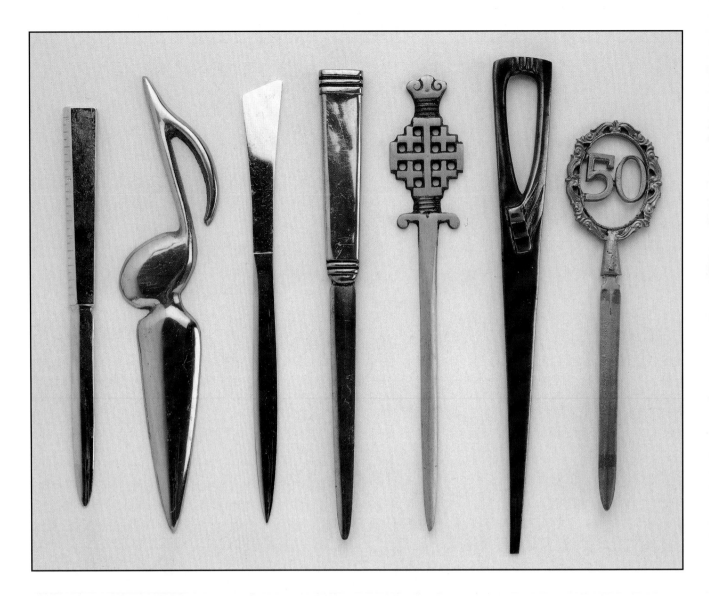

Plate 24. Left to right.

Brass

Ruler with three inches (3"), monogram "J" $8.00
Music note, Solid brass, USA $8.00
Two tone, plain $4.00
Plain $6.00
Celtic cross, Israel $5.00
Abstract $5.00
Brass colored metal, "50" in frame $4.00

Plate 25. Top to bottom.

BRASS

Knight in armor	$8.00
Lion on wall, Belgium	$10.00
Pineapple	$6.00
Unicorn	$15.00
Parrot	$12.00
Owl	$10.00
Lincoln head penny, two sided	$8.00

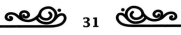

Plate 26. Left to right.

BRASS — MARKED CHINA

Lizard $10.00
Fish $10.00
Hammered abstract $6.00
Bird with flowers $10.00
Lizard $10.00
Flowers $8.00
Siam dancing god $10.00

Plate 27. Left to right.

BRASS — MARKED INDIA

Oval framed lion's head $12.00
Minerva $15.00
Plant $8.00
Knight $10.00
Pineapple on handle $8.00

Plate 28. Left to right.

BRASS — MARKED INDIA

Baccus $8.00
Rose $8.00
Bird $8.00
Camel neck and head $10.00
Pisces $8.00
Anchor $8.00

Plate 29. Left to right.

BRASS — MARKED INDIA

Flowers $8.00
Parrot $8.00
Bird $10.00
Oriental devil $10.00
Minerva $10.00
Knight $10.00
Bell with red, white, and blue stars, paper tag, Brassware from India by Sarna, 1952 . . . .$15.00

Plate 30. Left to right.

BRASS — MARKED INDIA

Red painted floral design $6.00
Heart $7.00
Red and blue enameled floral design $8.00
Indian god $10.00
Indian god $10.00
Oval framed lion's head $12.00
Pegasus $15.00

Plate 31. Left to right.

MISCELLANEOUS METALS

Cast aluminum, abstract $3.00
Silver plate and steel, made by International Silver, floral $5.00
Steel, geometric design $4.00
Steel, Olympic torch $5.00
Steel, made in Italy, Danesl Milano, Enzomari 1962, twist design $4.00
Pewter, Norway, #210, geometric $4.00
Red and white plastic and steel, Italy $4.00
Steel, floral design $4.00

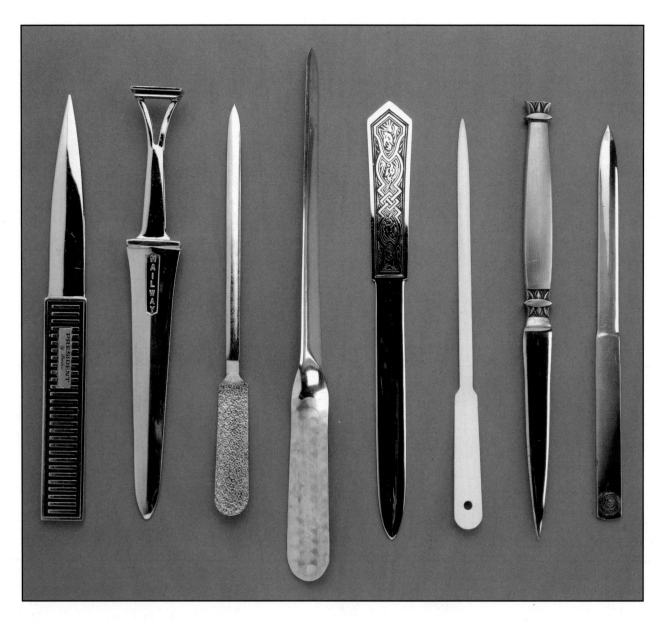

Plate 32. Left to right.

MISCELLANEOUS METALS

Chrome steel, President by Peerles, Japan $5.00
White metal, letter holder in handle, Mailway $6.00
Steel, ivy design $4.00
Steel, Auesta $4.00
Steel, dragon's head in geometric design, Italy $8.00
Off-white painted steel, Rodgers, Taiwan $3.00
Stainless steel, Japan $7.00
Chrome, University of Tenn., Knoxville $6.00

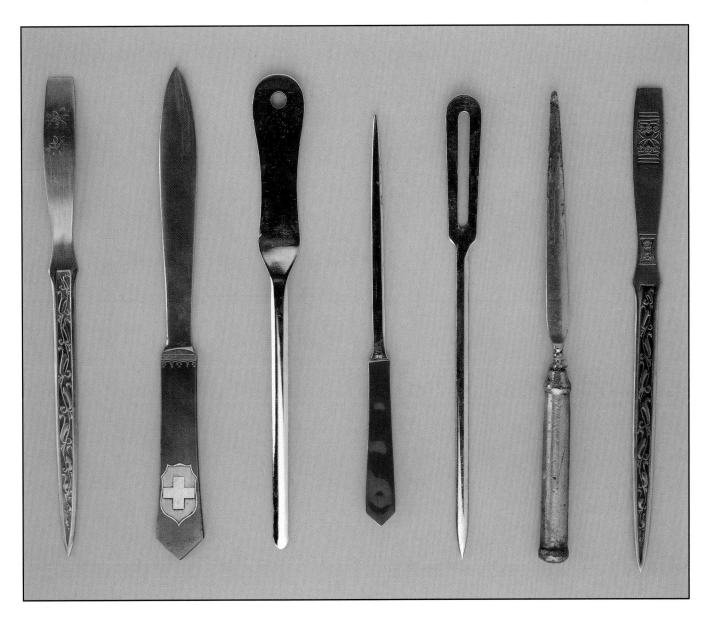

Plate 33. Left to right.

MISCELLANEOUS METALS

Stainless steel, floral, Japan $7.00
Steel, Siam enameling technique, cross and shield $20.00
Steel, plain, Japan $3.00
Blue and white, plastic and steel, Italy $3.00
Steel $3.00
White metal $4.00
Stainless steel, Japan, floral $8.00

Plate 34. Left to right.

M ISCELLANEOUS M ETALS

Bronze, pheasant $8.00
Brass, pheasant, H. K. Austria $35.00
Brass, colored steel, two horses with jockeys $15.00
Brass, chicken foot and feathers $15.00
Gold colored metal, cannon $4.00
Brass, two pheasants $20.00
Brass, animal character, Steinkjer $15.00
Brass, six inch (6") ruler, Italy, chariot design $8.00
Brass, three owls $12.00

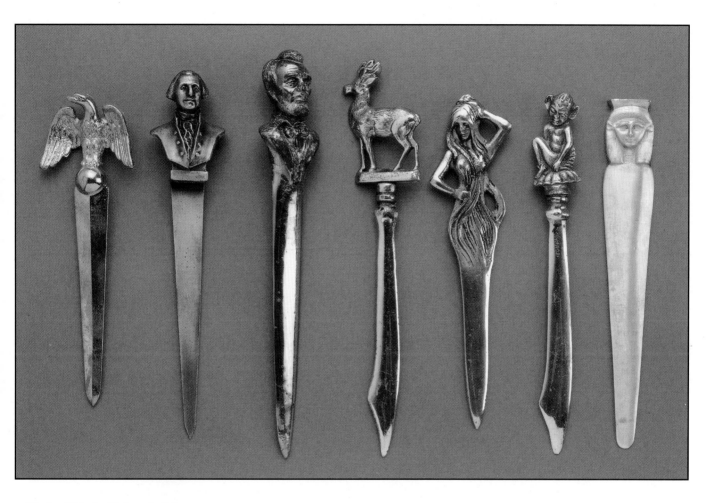

Plate 35. Left to right.

MISCELLANEOUS METALS

Gold-plated metal, eagle $8.00
Brass, George Washington's bust, Souvenir of Washington, D. C., made in USA by K.N.D. Co. .$12.00
Bronze colored metal, bust of Abe Lincoln, Dodge, Inc. $12.00
Brass, stag, England $12.00
Brass, Lady Godiva $15.00
Brass, imp, Lombard, England $12.00
Gold-plated metal, Egyptian head, MMA 1976 . . . .$10.00

Plate 36. Top to bottom.

MISCELLANEOUS METALS

Bronze-colored metal and stainless steel, pelican, Gulf Shores $8.00
Bronze, dragon motif, Shirokiya, Japan $12.00
Blackened steel, chicken's foot and feathers $8.00
Cast metal, knight in armor $12.00
Bronze, griffin over lion head $12.00
Brass and pewter, griffin over lion head $12.00

Plate 37. Left to right.

MISCELLANEOUS METALS

Pewter, dancing frog, Metzke 1979 . . . .$12.00
Pewter and brass, Carnival, New Orleans, Rex 1902 . . . .$20.00
Cast-bronze-colored metal, Old Slave Market, Charleston, S. C. $12.00
Bronze, Indian chief, Souvenir of Niagara Falls $35.00
Bronze, dragon with erotic scene on blade $35.00
Bronze-colored metal, woman with vase $18.00
Brass, abstract $8.00

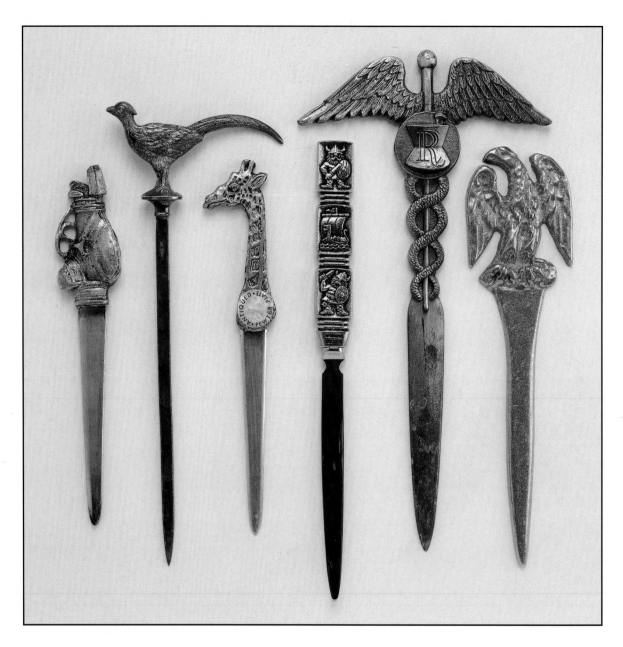

Plate 38. Left to right.

MISCELLANEOUS METALS

White metal, golf clubs and bag $15.00
Some silver content, II CCD, bird hallmark, pheasant $25.00
Pewter plate, giraffe, Metzke 1976 ....$10.00
Pewter, Stepttinn, three Viking scenes $8.00
White metal, caduceus with Rexall symbol $25.00
Pewter, early, eagle $10.00

Plate 39. Left to right.

MISCELLANEOUS METALS

White metal, golf clubs and bag, Metzke 1985 . . . .$15.00
Brass with green antiquing, palm tree, Israel $6.00
Pewter plate, sand dollar, Metzke $6.00
Silver-painted white metal, horse shoe with Kentucky and horse, Kentucky souvenir $8.00
Brass and steel, Charlemagne, Germany $25.00
Silver plate, Napoleon over French eagle $18.00
Gold plated, eagle on column $10.00
Pewter, fish, pewter image $8.00
Brass, bust of President Monroe $15.00
Brass and silver plate, fleur-de-lis, made in Birmingham $8.00
Copper, sword fish, Florida, made in Japan $8.00

Plate 40. Left to right.

MISCELLANEOUS METALS

Pewter plate, buffalo, M $10.00
Nickel, fleur-de-lis, Italy $6.00
Steel, Norwegian dragon, T. H. Krystad, Norway $15.00
Copper-colored pot metal, bust of Abe Lincoln, Peale Memorial Park, Gettysburg, Pa. $12.00
Pewter, Norwegian dragon, Pewter, Norway $20.00
Copper colored, rose motif $12.00
White metal, End of the Trail $10.00

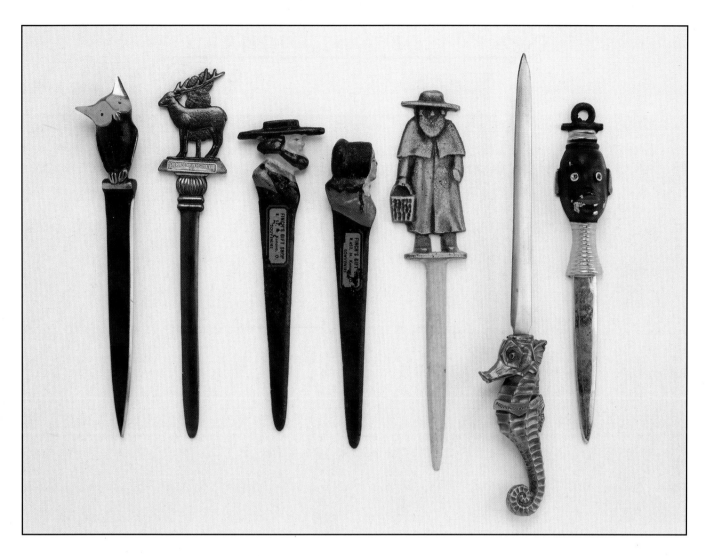

Plate 41. Left to right.

MISCELLANEOUS METALS

Brass, owl, Austria $15.00
Copper-colored metal, stag with tree, Cherokee Indian Reservation, N. C., Japan $10.00
Cast iron, Amish man, North Kenova, Oh, Finch's Gift Shop $20.00
Cast iron, Amish woman, North Kenova, Oh., Finch's Gift Shop $20.00
Off white and black painted cast aluminum, Amish man with basket, Penn. Dutch Gifts,
    Lancaster, Pa. $25.00
Bronze, sea horse, Province Town, Mass. $18.00
Gold and black-colored pot metal, head of black girl $25.00

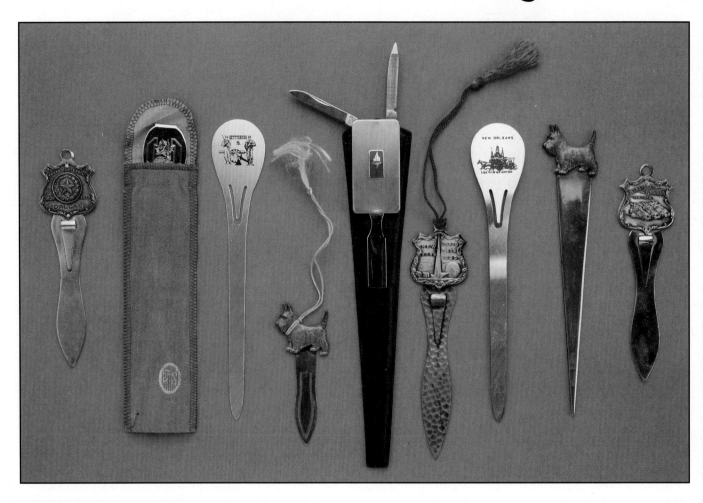

Plate 42. Left to right.

BOOKMARKS

Steel, Texas Centennial, Dallas $6.00
Brass, Oriental Dragon inside Block "C" with green cloth sheath, stamped F.S. $12.00
Brass color, Gettysburg, Pa. $4.00
Copper, Scottie with green tassel leash $10.00
Steel, nail file, pen knife combo, torch logo in plastic sheath, marked
     Imperial Stainless, U.S.A. $12.00
Bronze color, New York World's Fair, 1939 . . . .$18.00
Brass color, New Orleans French Quarter $4.00
Copper, Scottie dog $12.00
Chrome color, Saratoga Springs, New York $15.00

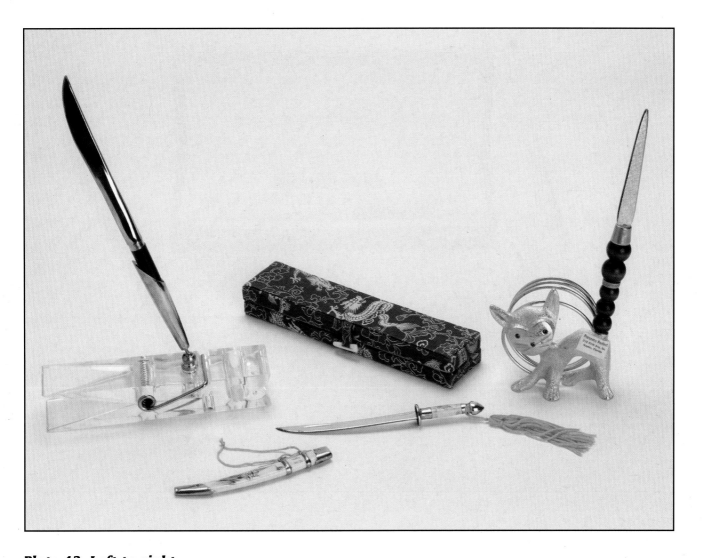

Plate 43. Left to right.

DESK SETS

Clear plastic and gold-tone metal, letter holder, paperweight pen, and letter opener $15.00
Silk dragon covered box, bone with bone tongue, steel and scrimshaw polyester,
    ceremonial knife $25.00
Gold plate and dark wood, cat letter holder with green rhinestone eyes and nose, pen
    and letter opener, Presents Perfect on paper label $18.00

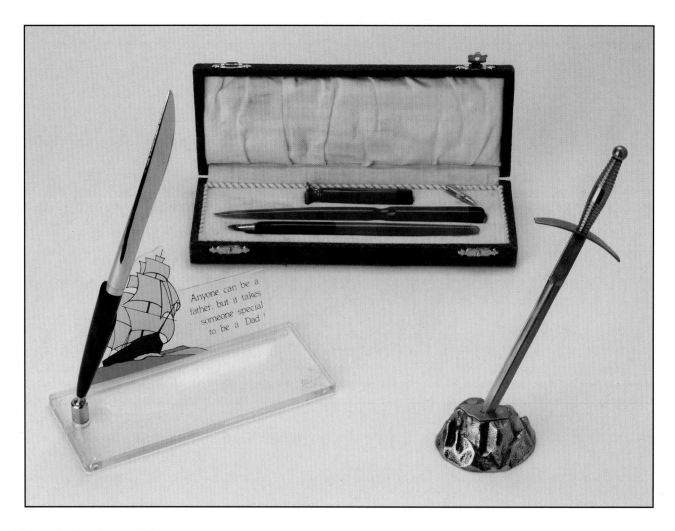

Plate 44. Left to right.

DESK SETS

Clear plastic, decal, black and silver plastic, pen, letter opener with ship plaque, gift
for Dad, marked J.S., N.Y., made in Hong Kong $8.00
Leatherette box, black and carnelian Bakelite, wax sealer, letter opener, pen with extra nib,
marked Fountain Pen Co., New York $95.00
Brass, represents sword and stone, paperweight and letter opener $15.00

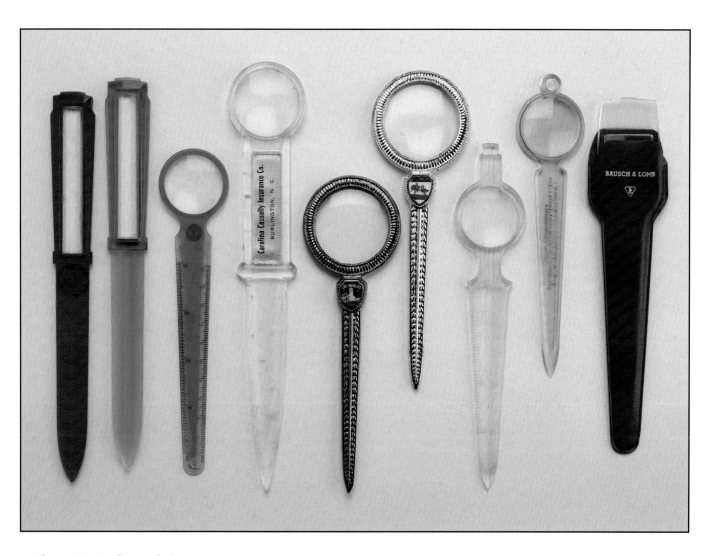

Plate 45. Left to right.

Magnifiers

Red plastic with brass shield, Annapolis, marked S.P., made in U.S.A. $6.00
Green plastic, marked S.P., made in U.S.A. $3.00
Yellow plastic, glass lens, ruler, magnifier, and letter opener, marked Bausch & Lomb
    Opt. Co., Rochester, N.Y. $3.00
Clear plastic, Carolina Casualty Insurance Co., Burlington, N. C. $3.00
Gold-tone pot metal, Los Angles, Calif. $3.00
Gold-tone pot metal, Florida $3.00
Clear plastic, also a ruler $3.00
Pink plastic, Enjoy Tomorrow's Plumbing & Heating Today the P & H Budget Plan Way $3.00
Clear plastic with red plastic sheath, also a ruler, Bausch & Lomb $3.00

Plate 46. Top to bottom.

MISCELLANEOUS

Celluloid, pencil in mouth of alligator, pencil has black boys head as top, marked
    Germany, Deposé $60.00
Celluloid and steel, mechanical pencil, Henry L. Genslinger $15.00
Plastic and steel, retractable blade, Ronald Reagan, Birthplace, Tampico, Il. $4.00
Carved wood, dip pen enclosed, wax sealer on top $25.00
Black plastic $3.00
Chrome, brass, and steel, paperweight shaped like a duck $12.00
Bronze, paperweight shaped like scales, marked Dayton International Business Machines,
    Edward Canley, 40th Anniversary, Dayton Scale Co., Dec. 9, 1930 . . . .$50.00
Plaster, letter opener, pen, and refill, pat. P. Royal $3.00

Plate 47. Left to right.

MISCELLANEOUS

Plastic and steel, fish handle, nail clipper and file, shield marked Missouri, with mule $10.00
Pewter, ruler, San Antonio, Texas, marked with a man holding a shield with an "E," and
    holding a sword $10.00
Steel, bottle opener, marked Muster Gschutzt, Engeht CIE Germany $8.00
Pewter, ruler, Clemson Tigers, marked with a man holding a shield with an "E," and
    holding a sword $10.00
Plastic and steel, toe nail clippers and file, New York City, marked Made in Hong Kong $10.00
Alpaca and abalone, coral eye, fish-shaped bottle opener $20.00

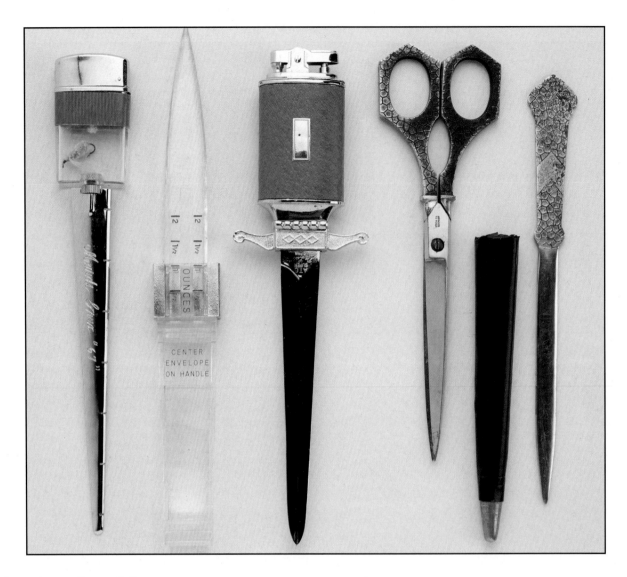

Plate 48. Left to right.

MISCELLANEOUS

Plastic and steel, cigarette lighter with fishing fly in body, ruler blade, Mardi Gras '67,
   Japan $40.00
Plastic and chromed brass, magnifier and letter weighing scales on blade from ½ to
   2 ounces, center envelope on handle, marked Stamp-Teller U.S.S., Patent Pending $18.00
Leather and chrome steel, lighter with monogram plaque, marked ATC Super De Lux,
   Japan $20.00
Nickel and steel, scissors and letter opener in black leather sheath, marked Utica Co.,
   Germany $30.00

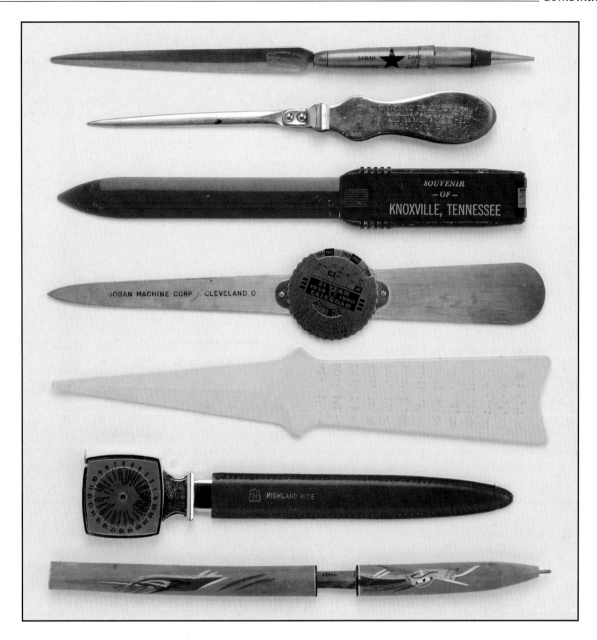

Plate 49. Top to bottom.

MISCELLANEOUS

Plastic, brass, and steel, pen, Owes Sarah Dake, 1953, Tarcia and Russell Peebles, Illiopolis,
Ill. $15.00
Chrome Steel, letter gripper, Citizens Trust Company, Broadway & Sumner Ave. and 198
Montague Street, Brooklyn, New York $18.00
Red plastic, Souvenir of Knoxville, Tennessee, handle has 1948–49 calendar insert $10.00
Steel, Gogan Machine Corp., Cleveland, O., with 21-year perpetual calendar,
1939–1960 with adjustments for leap year $15.00
Beige plastic, Braille alphabet $10.00
Leather and chrome, 4 ft. tape measure, leather sheath, Dial for World Time in Major
Cities, sheath marked Highland Hide, blade marked Stainless Steel, Japan $15.00
Painted wood and steel, pen, knife, Japan, marked Avril, Inc. — Detergents and Sanitizers,
E. Guilday, Wash., D.C., D1 7-5231 . . . .$10.00

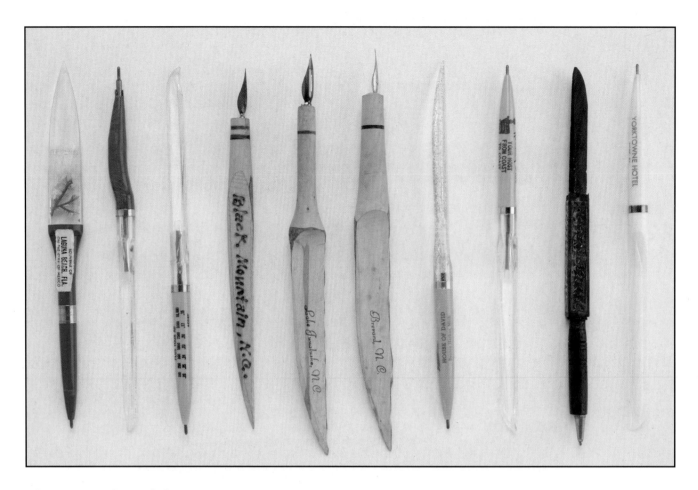

Plate 50. Left to right.

PENS

Plastic and brass, pen and magnifier, Souvenir of Laguna Beach, Fla. on the Gulf of Mexico . .$12.00
Plastic, pen, magnifier, ruler, made in U.S.A. $3.00
Plastic, pen, magnifier, ruler, a print advertisement, made in U.S.A. $3.00
Wood dip pen, Black Mountain, N.C. . . . .$ 6.00
Wood dip pen, Lake Junaluska, N.C. . . . .$ 6.00
Wood dip pen, Brevard, N.C. $6.00
Plastic, train motif, House of David, Benton Harbor, Mich. $3.00
Plastic, ruler, pen, and magnifier, Holiday Inn, Your Host from Coast to Coast $3.00
Teakwood and brass $8.00
Plastic, pen and ruler, Yorktown Hotel, Yorktown, Pa. $3.00

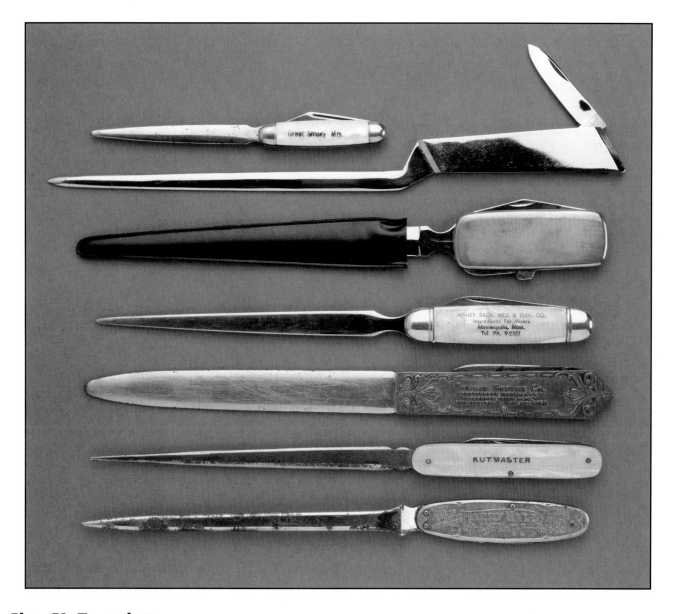

Plate 51. Top to bottom.

PEN KNIVES

Plastic and steel, Great Smoky Mts., knife blade, Imperial U.S.A. $10.00
Steel, blade, Inck, made in France $8.00
Brass and steel, knife/scissors combo, plastic sheath, Stainless, China $12.00
Celluloid and steel, Maney Bros. Mill and Elev. Co., Minneapolis, Minn., on blade — I.K.O.C.,
    U.S.A. $18.00
Bronze and steel, Borman Service Co., Philadelphia, Remington U.M.C., U.S.A. on blade $85.00
Celluloid and steel, W. C. Morris & Assoc., Kutmaster, Blade, Kutmaster,
    Uttica, N.Y., U.S.A. on reverse $25.00
Steel, Harry Hall, Tailords Ad., Cheapside $30.00

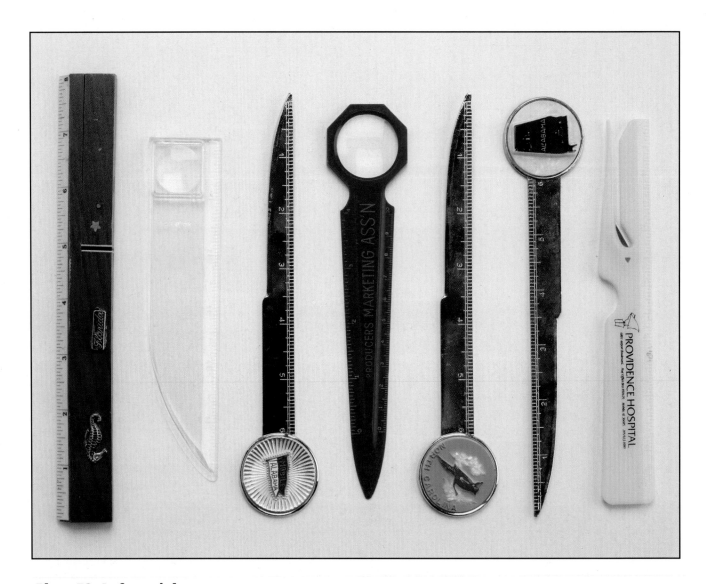

Plate 52. Left to right.

RULERS

Wood, plastic, brass, and steel, ruler, knife, Florida, blade Stainless Steel, Japan $10.00
Plastic, ruler, magnifier, and tracing curve, Hong Kong $3.00
Steel, ruler, Mobile, Alabama, marked with a soldier with a sword and shield marked "E" $4.00
Plastic, magnifier/ruler, Producers Marketing, Ass'n. $3.00
Steel, North Carolina, marked on reverse with a soldier with a sword and shield marked "E" . .$4.00
Steel, Alabama, marked on reverse with a soldier with a sword and shield marked "E" $4.00
Plastic, Providence Hospital, Mobile, AL $3.00

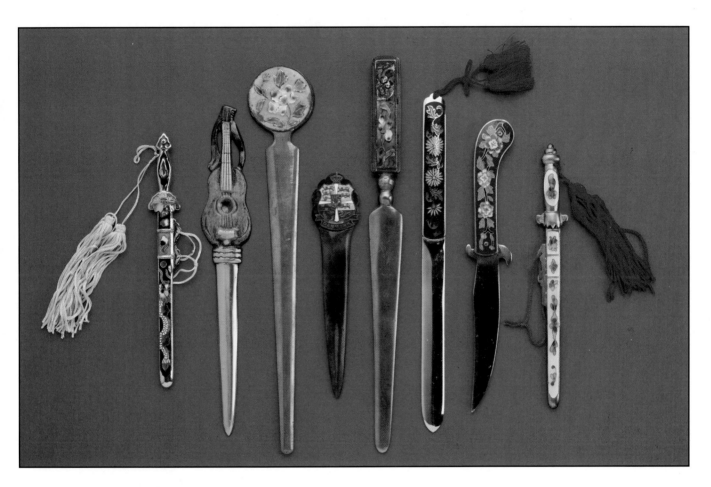

Plate 53. Left to right.

Enamel and chrome, dragon motif, green tassel $25.00
Brass, Made in Israel $8.00
Enameld brass, China, flower motif $15.00
Bronze and enamel, marked Argentor Bronce, Denmark $25.00
Enamel and brass, flower motif, China $20.00
Enamel and steel, yellow flowers, red tassel $15.00
Enamel, brass, and steel, blue and yellow flowers $25.00
Enamel and brass, flower motif, red tassel $30.00

Plate 54. Left to right.

Silver plate $5.00
Silver plate $5.00
Gold tone, dangling bust of Lincoln, Good Luck $5.00
Pewter, Metzaks 1984, auto $8.00
Genuine alligator head and wood, souvenir of Clark Hill Dam, S.C. $25.00
Bakelite, Germany $50.00
Gold tone, Sunshine State, Fla. $10.00
Brass, Norge, Norheimsund $8.00
Copper colored, enamel, and steel, Good Luck $8.00
Copper, Souvenir Orlando, Fla., Abbot Wares, Los Angeles $15.00

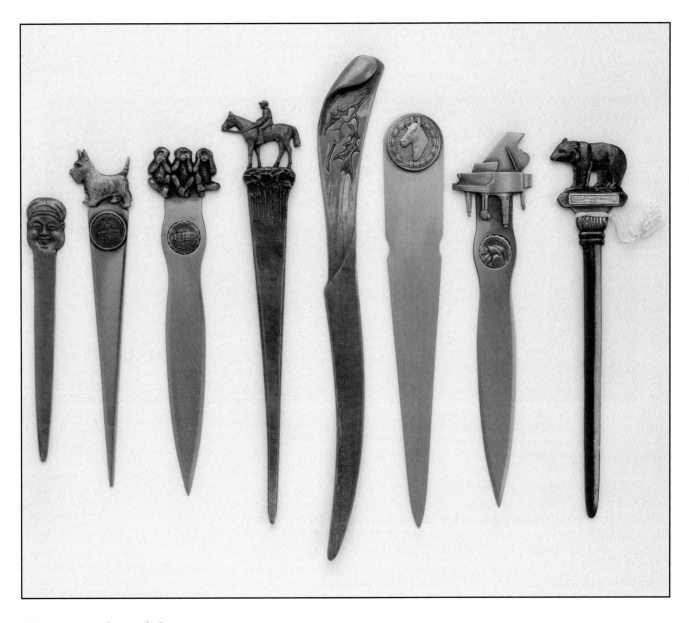

Plate 55. Left to right.

Brass, smiling Chinese elder $15.00
Copper, State Capitol, Atlanta, Ga., Scottie $10.00
Copper, Coliseum, Evansville, Ind., three monkeys $10.00
Bronze, back marked Jockey $45.00
Brass, Art Nouveau, holly motif $30.00
Copper, horse head $12.00
Copper, Mammoth Cave, Kentucky, piano $10.00
Copper color, foil label, Cherokee Indian Reservation, N.C., bear, made in Japan $10.00

Plate 56. Left to right.

Gold-colored pot metal, lobster $8.00
Gold-colored pot metal, pineapple, Hawaii $5.00
Gold-colored pot metal, trout, Arkansas the Wonder State $8.00
Silver, Smoky the Bear, Prevent Forest Fires, Itasca State Park, Minn., marked Silver Holland .$45.00
Gold-colored pot metal, bronco buster, San Antonio, Tex., The Alamo $8.00
Copper and steel, owl $6.00
Gold-tone pot metal and enamel, Aloha from Hawaii $4.00
Gold-color pot metal, sea horse and fish, Fla. $6.00
Pewter, herd of elephants, marked Metzke 1980 . . . .$6.00
Pot metal and brass, flower bouquet $6.00
Pewter plate, butterfly, marked Metzke 1975 . . . .$6.00

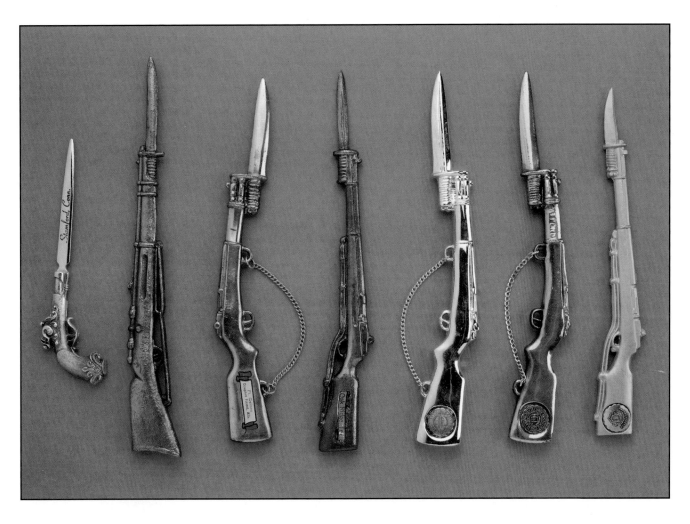

Plate 57. Left to right.

Brass, Derringer, Stamford, Ct. $10.00
Bronze-colored pot metal, Memphis, Tn. $6.00
Brass, Ft. Gaines, Dauphin Island, Al. $8.00
Bronze-colored pot metal, Oak Ridge, Tn. $6.00
Gold plated, Old Spanish Fort, Pascagoula, Miss. $8.00
Gold plated, Alabama Polytechnic Institution $6.00
Gold painted, Mass. $6.00

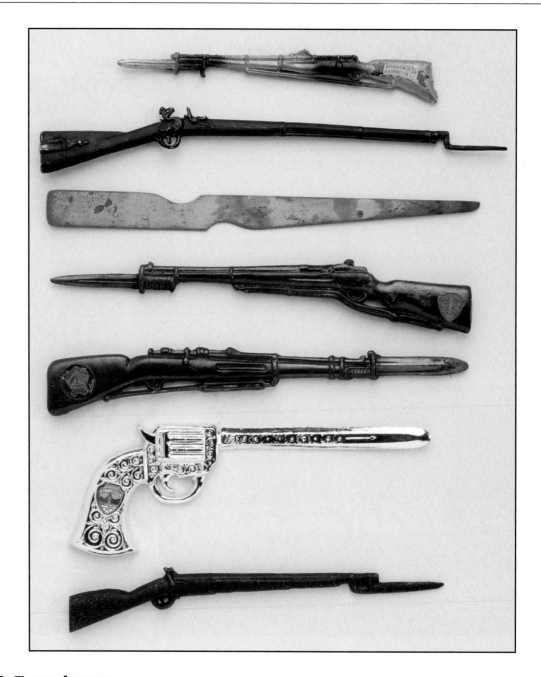

Plate 58. Top to bottom.

Copper color, Washington, D. C. $8.00
Cast iron, sold as a paperweight, letter opener at Gettysburg, Pa., Centennial of Civil War . . .$18.00
Brass, marked Bradley & Hubbard, Mfg. $35.00
Gun-metal color, New York $10.00
Bronze color, Springfield, Ill. $10.00
Silver-plated pot metal and enamel, Gettysburg, Pa. $10.00
Cast iron rifle $10.00

Plate 59. Left to right.

Tortoise shell with 3-D bird's claw holding a movable tortoise marble, Victorian $125.00
Horn, whale with ivory eye, Hawaii $25.00
Horn, Philippines $25.00
Horn, intricately engraved, house and beach motif, Flowers and Word, Philippines $45.00
Antler, dark and blond horn, Brainard, Minn. $45.00
Horn, Taiwan $15.00
Sterling, tortoise, Egyptian Hallmark and No. 30 . . . .$50.00
Mottled tortoise, elephant head motif, Santo Domingo, Victorian $85.00

Plate 60. Left to right.

Small, fancy cut-outs in handle $30.00
Ivory and ebony $35.00
Egyptian god $50.00
Pierce and turned design handle, bone blade, painted design, Mexico $75.00
Silver and ivory, Art Nouveau swallow motif on handle, Victorian $125.00
Alpaca and abalone, bottle opener $30.00
Silver plate with Delft plaque, marked GE HA, Made in Holland $10.00
French ivory, Mille Lacs, Indian Trading Post, Onamia, Minn. $15.00
Abalone, Chinatown, San Francisco, Calif. $10.00

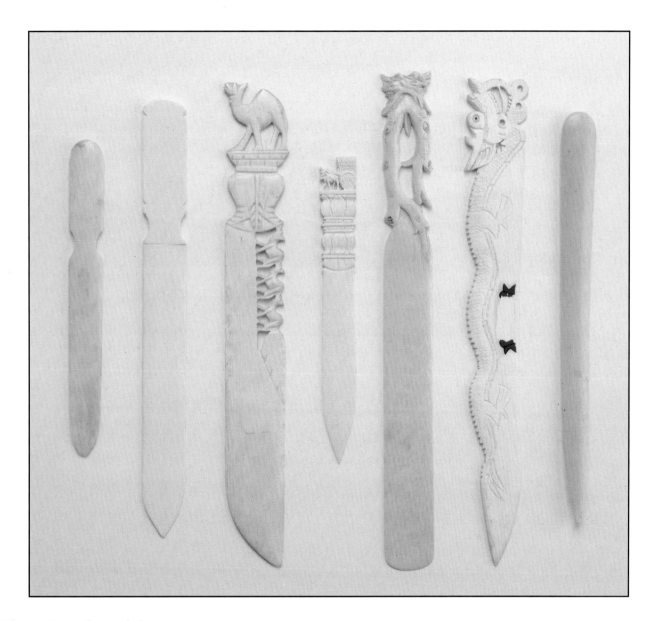

Plate 61. Left to right.

Dragon motif on reverse side of handle $25.00
Plain $30.00
Carved camel motif $60.00
Carved burro pulling wagon $40.00
Branch motif, Victorian $90.00
Carved dragon motif, double sided $55.00
French ivory, plain $10.00

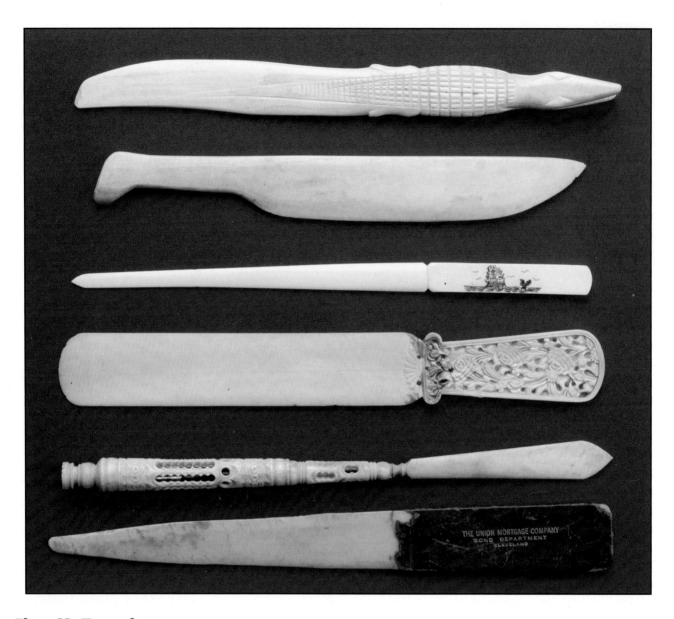

Plate 62. Top to bottom.

Carved crocodile $85.00
Bone, plain $20.00
Scrimshaw of schooner and bird $45.00
Intricately carved floral design on front, back has intricately carved Chinese box weave
    design and was mended at break between handle and blade with sterling plate with
    six pins. Repair appears to be from Victorian era. $125.00
Bone, intricately carved with dip pin in handle, wax seal on top $55.00
Leather and French ivory, The Union Mortgage Co., Cleveland, stamped B & B on handle $10.00

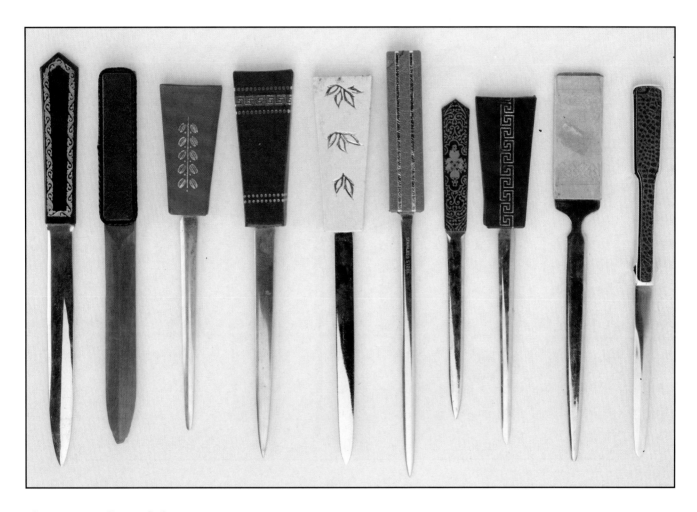

Plate 63. Left to right.

Brown leather with gold stamp, marked Italy $6.00
Brown leather with black braided border and wood blade $6.00
Green leather with gold stamp, made in U.S.A. $6.00
Red leather with gold stamp $6.00
Creme leather with gold stamp $6.00
Orange leather with gold stamp $6.00
Maroon leather with gold, orange, and green flower motif, Germany $8.00
Maroon with gold stamp, made in U.S.A. $6.00
Beige with gold stamp $6.00
Crocodile skin insert, marked Carvel Hall, Stainless, U.S.A. $6.00

Plate 64. Left to right.

Butterscotch Bakelite, hand-painted flowers, Ocean City, Md. $25.00
Yellow marble Bakelite handle, silver, brass collar, nickel blade, Chicago World's Fair, 1934 .$75.00
Butterscotch Bakelite, reverse painted glass inset, Souvenir Montgomery, Al. $20.00
Lucite handle, carved and reverse painted fish, Hot Springs, Arkansas $15.00
Celluloid Art Deco handle, ca 1920's $10.00
Butterscotch Bakelite handle, hand-painted flowers, Green Mountain, Vt. $25.00
Lucite with stag in handle $12.00
Black and transparent Bakelite with encapsulated sea horse $20.00
Bullet celluloid handle, Vanderbilt Commodores $12.00
Lucite handle with glitter and brass fillings $18.00
Lucite handle in shape of fish, encapsulated seashells, Souvenir of Mississippi $35.00
Butterscotch Bakelite handle, hand-painted palm tree motif, Ocala, Fl. $25.00

Plate 65. Left to right.

Lucite, three U.S. pennies, paper label, Unique, Canada $15.00
Lucite, 1968 Canadian coins, penny, nickel, and dime, Unique, Canada $15.00
Lucite, encapsulated decal, New York City, gold metal Statue of Liberty, with dyed shells
    and mica chips $12.00
Lucite, three 1960 U.S. pennies, Sturbridge Candy & Gift Shoppe $18.00
Lucite, two 1976 U.S. pennies, Las Vegas $12.00
Lucite, encapsulated gold leaf, Victoria, B.C.. . . . .$12.00

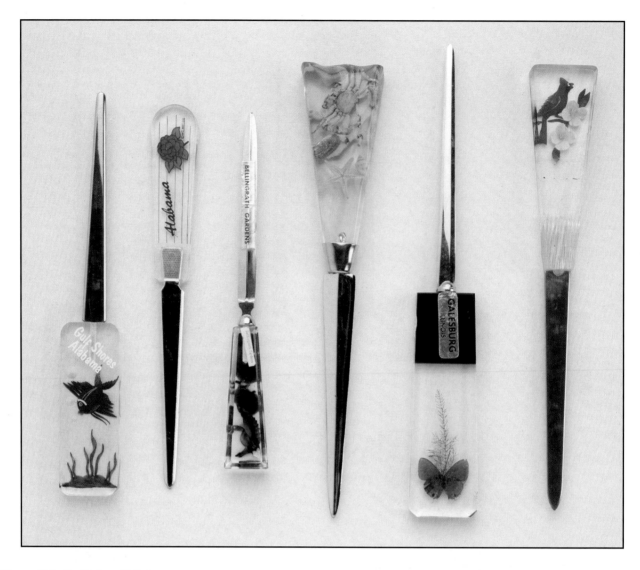

Plate 66. Left to right.

Lucite, reverse carved painted fish, Gulf Shores, Alabama $15.00
Plastic, Alabama, M.C. Art Co. $8.00
Lucite, with wild duck scene in handle, two paper labels, Bellingrath Gardens $20.00
Lucite with encapsulated crab, coral, seashells, and starfish $35.00
Lucite, encapsulated pressed moth and fern, Galesburg, Illinois, made in Canada $18.00
Lucite, reverse carved and filled cardinal and flowers, additional carving on handle,
    paper lable, Bircraft Trademark, hand carved and colored, very desirable brand $30.00

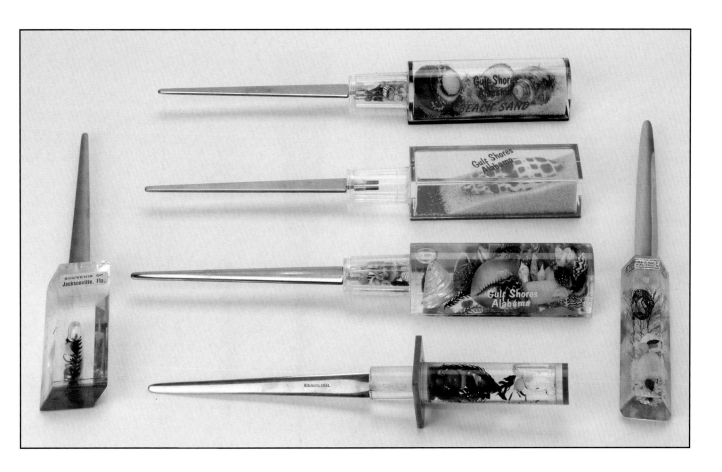

Plate 67. Top to bottom.

Plastic, hollow handle with seashells and white sand, Gulf Shores, Alabama Beach Sand $18.00
Plastic, hollow handle with fancy seashell and white sand, Gulf Shores, Alabama $15.00
Plastic, hollow handle, liquid filled with seashells and seaweed, Gulf Shores, Alabama $25.00
Plastic, hollow handle, liquid filled with dyed seashells, seaweed, and genuine sea horse . . .$20.00

Left side.
Lucite, liquid filled compartment with shells, seaweed, and genuine sea horse,
    Souvenir, Jacksonville, Fla. $15.00

Right side.
Lucite handle, shells, seaweed, and sea horse, Florida Gulf Arium, Ft. Walton Beach $18.00

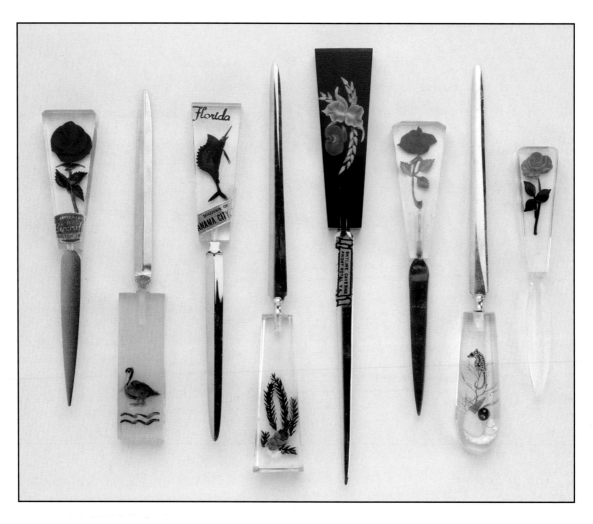

Plate 68. Left to right.

Lucite, reverse carved and filled rose, Bircraft label, very desirable $30.00
Lucite, reverse carved and painted pelican $18.00
Lucite, reverse carved and filled Florida, Souvenir of Panama City, Fla. $25.00
Lucite, encapsulated seaweed, hemlock pine cone, and shell chips $15.00
Lucite with flowers, Skyline Caverns, Front Royal, Va. $25.00
Lucite, reverse carved and filled rose $20.00
Lucite, encapsulated seashells, seaweed, and sea horse $15.00
Lucite, reverse carved and filled rose, magnifier blade $25.00

ᘒᕯᔦ Miscellaneous

Plate 69. Left to right.

Steel opener with hand-painted camel bone plaque, scene from India with tiger and antelope . .$25.00
Silver, pierced work floral handle, hand engraved, V. S. Bergen, marked 830 Silver, L. A.,
 Victorian $65.00
Silver plate, figural man and lamb, The Good Shepherd, Vatican Pavilion, New York
 World's Fair, 1964–65, marked E.P.N.S., TH. Marthinsen, Norway $25.00
Silver and celluloid, raised owl handle, marked on blade, Tore, stamped 830 Silver, M&M . . .$45.00
Sterling and enamel, Victoria's crest, stamped Sterling, Victorian $45.00
Bronze, 50th Anniversary, Brown and Bieglow $25.00
Sterling and tortoise, inset tortoise handle with inlaid sterling wire, British hallmarks on
 back, Victorian $85.00

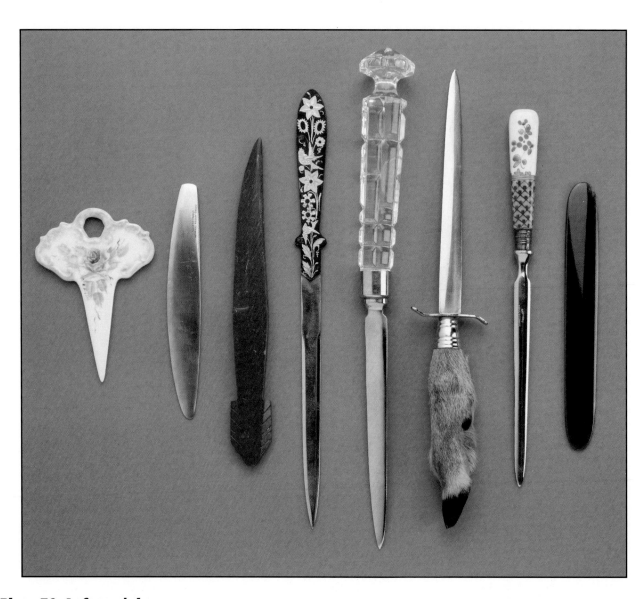

Plate 70. Left to right.

Hand-painted porcelain, rose motif, signed R. Riddle $45.00
Stainless steel, marked Georg Jensen, Denmark $25.00
Carved jasper $35.00
Japanese damascene $35.00
Full lead crystal, signed Godinger, West Germany $65.00
European deer hoof handle $15.00
Hand-painted porcelain handle, sterling collar with British hallmark, blade marked
    Stainless Steel, England $35.00
Jadeite $85.00

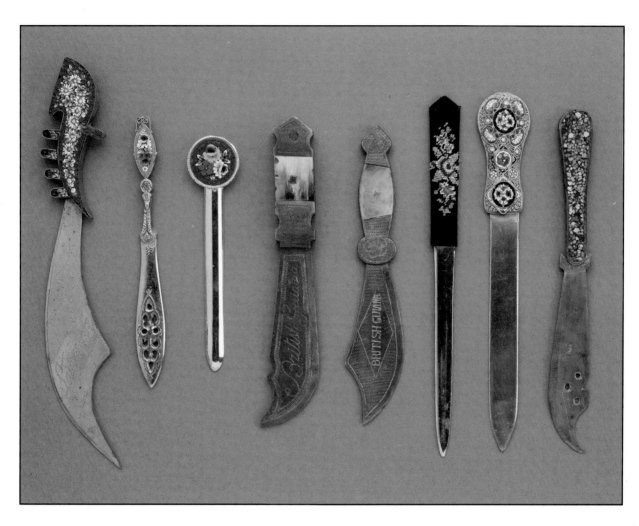

Plate 71. Left to right.

Brass, souvenir, exceptional small pieces indicating older piece $85.00
Silver plate, pierced blade $25.00
Gold plate $15.00
Brass & blond Horn, British Guiana $30.00
Brass & blond Horn, British Guiana $30.00
Steel with needlepoint handle, Germany $25.00
Brass, very fine pieces, intricate design, very desirable, stamped made in Italy, FAP $75.00
Brass & turquoise, made in India $15.00

Plate 72. Left to right.

Plain $15.00
Hand-painted orange & blossoms, Jacksonville, Fla. $15.00
Hand-painted orange & blossoms, Jacksonville, Fla. $15.00
Carved, Victorian $65.00
Sterling handle, Art Nouveau, Victorian $70.00
Carved wooden alligator handle, Souvenir of Florida $45.00
Silverware brass handle, floral openwork, Victorian $50.00
Bronze, open work handle, Arc de Triomphe, DE L ETOILE $35.00

Plate 73. Left to right.

Brass, bird headed dragon $12.00
Brass, abstract religious motif, marked copyright, Terra Sancta Guild 1969, Israel $8.00
Gold colored pot metal, red 40 . . . .$6.00
Brass, diamond shapes, marked KL1803 Israel $8.00
Brass, Hallmark with two men $12.00
Brass, Wien $8.00
Brass, dove of peace and olive branch, clean air, land & water, marked Terra Sancta
    Guild 1970, Israel $8.00
Brass, bird and peace, marked Terra Sancta Guild 1968, Israel $8.00
Brass, Abstract $6.00

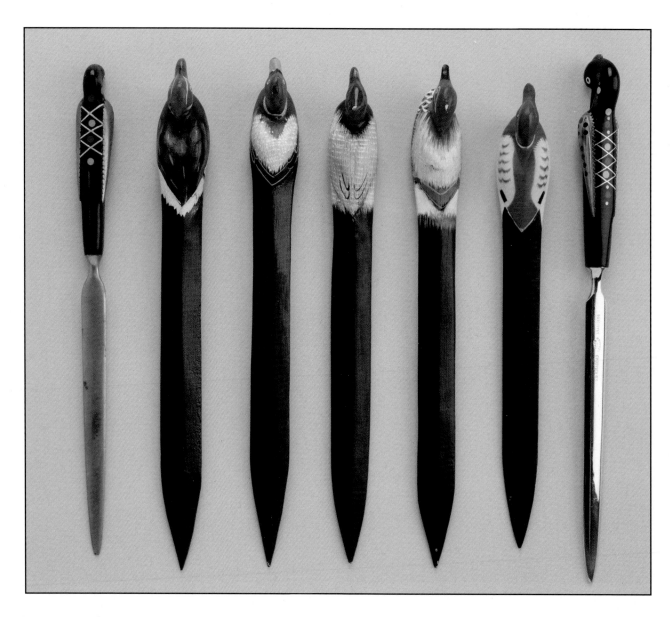

Plate 74. Left to right.

Bakelite, brass, and aluminum, inlaid with bits of colored Bakelite & aluminum wire $35.00
Wood Duck, copyright 1987 Dakin, Inc., San Francisco, product of China $8.00
Wood Duck, copyright 1987 Dakin, Inc., San Francisco, product of China $8.00
Wood Duck, copyright 1987 Dakin, Inc., San Francisco, product of China $8.00
Wood Duck, copyright 1987 Dakin, Inc., San Francisco, product of China $8.00
Wood Duck, copyright 1987 Dakin, Inc., San Francisco, product of China $8.00
Bakelite, brass & aluminum, inlaid with bits of colored Bakelite & aluminum wire, made in
    Lebanon S & A Haddad, stainless $45.00

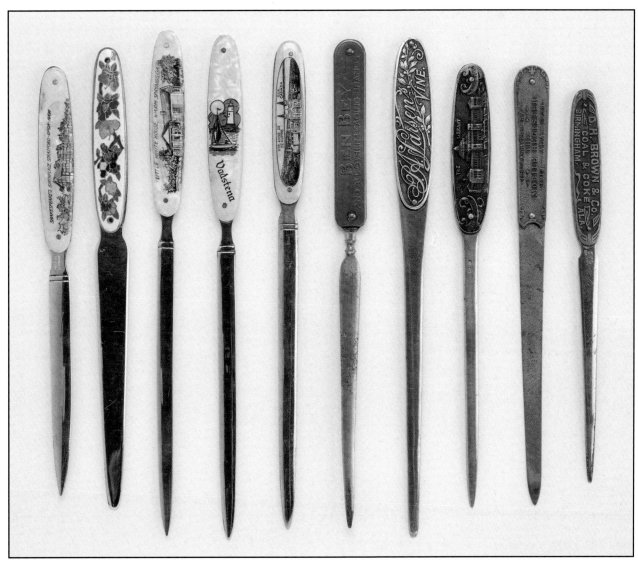

Plate 75. Left to right.

Celluloid & steel, Shakespeare's birthplace, Stratford-upon-Avon, made in Germany $25.00
Cloisonné enamel, brass and steel $20.00
Celluloid & steel, Little White House, Warm Springs, Ga., made in Germany $40.00
Celluloid & steel, Vadstena, made in Germany $25.00
Celluloid & steel, Ste. Anne De Beaupre, Que. Canada $25.00
Brass & steel, Ben Bey and all other leading brands, 83 W. Randolph St. $30.00
Aluminum & steel, P. A. Larsen's Vine $25.00
Steel on front, Greeting The Library Washington, stamped Germany, The Capitol,
        Washington on reverse, stamped Magnetic Cuttery C2, Phila., Pa. $30.00
Brass & steel, letter opener & fingernail file, 125th Anniversary, The Mobile Register,
        1813 - Ala. - 1938 . . . .$30.00
Brass & steel, D.H. Brown & Co., Coal & Coke, Birmingham, Ala., stamped "Antelope"
        on reverse, H. Keschner, Solingen, Germany $30.00

Plate 76. Left to right.

WOOD

Old woman, Quebec, Canada $25.00
Old woman, also bookmark, Aude $20.00
Old man with hat, Great Smoky Mtns. $25.00
Royal Canadian Mounted Police, Windsor, Canada $35.00
Swedish bloak, Handarbete, made in Sweden $25.00
Man in red hat $25.00

Plate 77. Left to right.

WOOD

Carved Indian chief $22.00
Northwestern Indian totem $12.00
Primitive carved and painted Indian $25.00
Northwestern Indian totem $10.00
Northwestern Indian totem $10.00
Primitive carved and painted Indian chief Quoddy Wig Wam, Perry, Maine $12.00
Hand-carved & painted Indian chief, The Chalet, Mt. Royal Park, Montreal, Canada $20.00

Plate 78. Left to right.

F<small>IGURALS</small>

Golfer, made in Italy $12.00
Owl, made in Italy, original $8.00
Scrimshawed polyester elephant $10.00
Owl, made in Italy $8.00

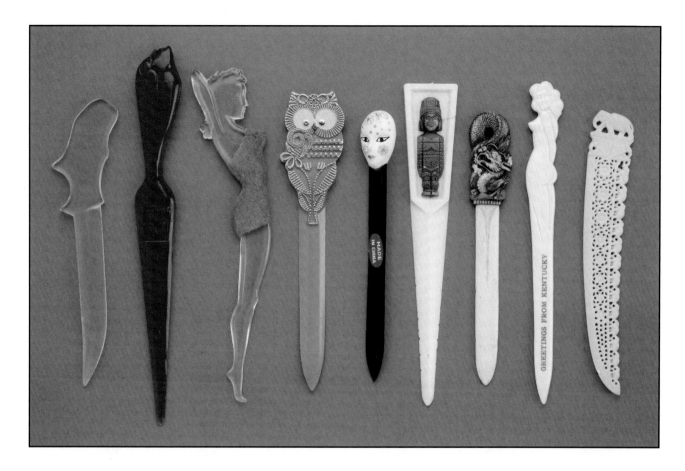

Plate 79. Left to right.

FIGURALS

Clear Lucite, unusual $12.00
Inland, Mfg. Div, GMC, depicts Chief Pontiac as used as hood ornaments $24.00
Bathing beauty with/flocked suit $20.00
Green owl $3.00
Double sided, hand-painted mask motif, made in China $4.00
Aztec god $4.00
Dragon $8.00
Nude, Greetings from Kentucky $8.00
Elephants $3.00

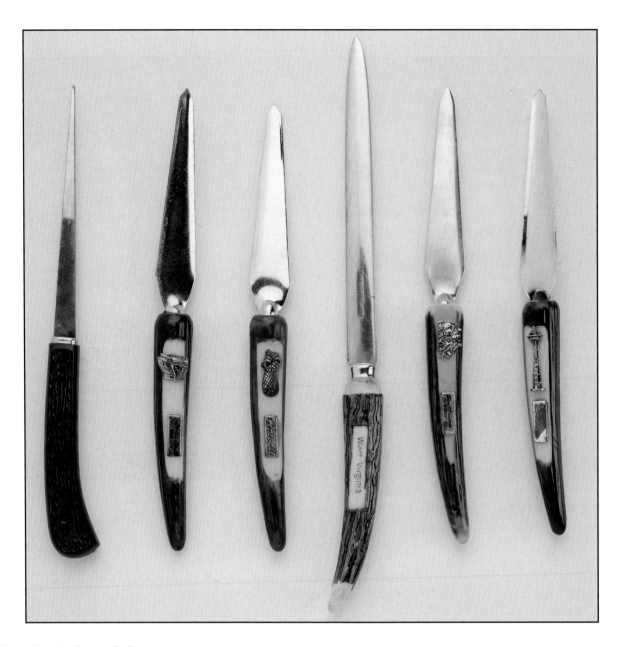

Plate 80. Left to right.

HANDLES

Plain, Greenville, Tn. $3.00
Lovers Leap, Rock City $4.00
Hawaii $4.00
West Virginia $4.00
Stone Mtn., Georgia $4.00
Seattle, Wash. $4.00

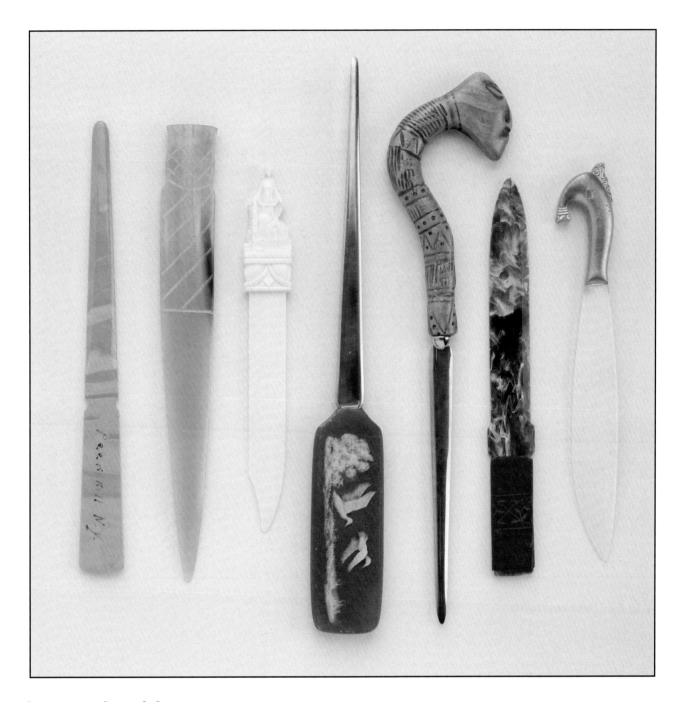

Plate 81. Left to right.

MISCELLANEOUS

Orange & yellow marblized Bakelite, Peekskill, N.Y. $25.00
Horn, tristle motif, Dykehead Horncraft, made in Scotland $18.00
National Shrine of the Immaculate Conception, Washington, DC, made in Italy $4.00
Ducks in flight, by Design Gifts International, U.S.A. $5.00
Mexican motif, made in U.S.A. $5.00
Leatherette handle $3.00
Abstract $3.00

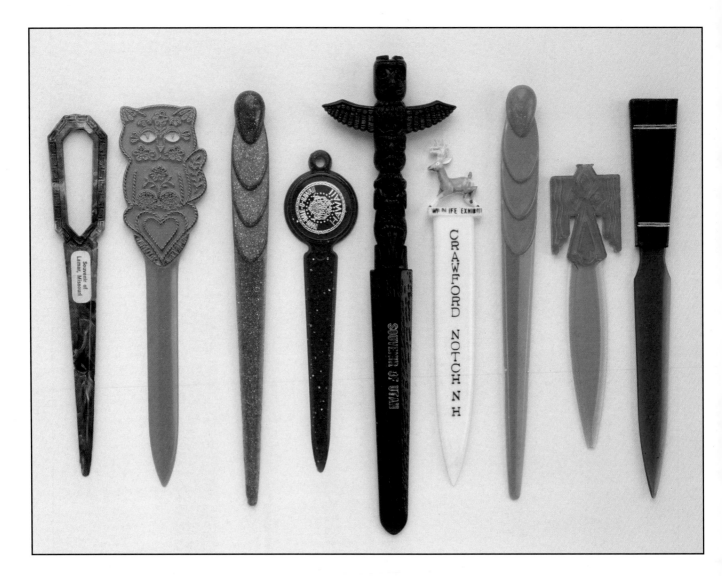

Plate 82. Left to right.

MISCELLANEOUS

Souvenirs of Lamar, Missouri $3.00
Cat $3.00
Abstract $3.00
Nani-Hale-O-Hawaii $3.00
Totem, souvenir of Utah $4.00
Stag, Wildlife Exhibit, Crawford Notch, NH $6.00
Abstract $3.00
Thunderbird $3.00
Leather handle $3.00

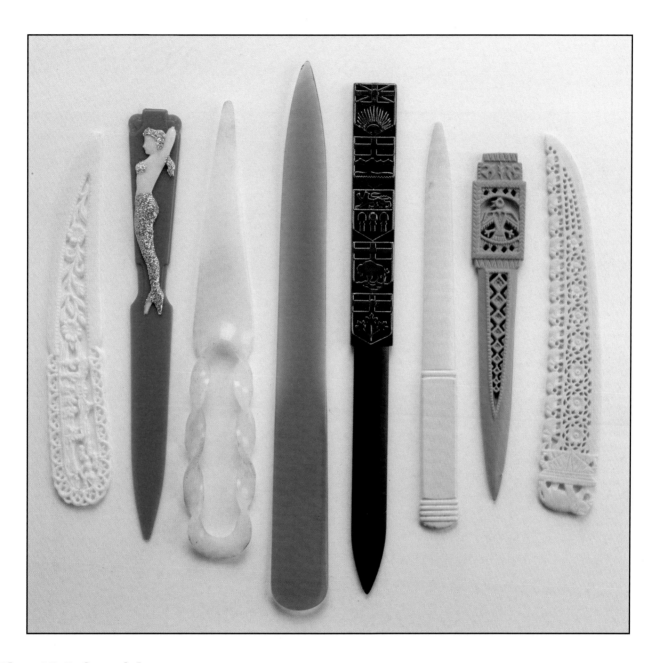

Plate 83. Left to right.

MISCELLANEOUS

Oriental design	$3.00
Mermaid, made in U.S.A.	$6.00
Twisted handle	$3.00
Green, plain	$3.00
Shield & crest	$3.00
Plain	$3.00
Thunderbird	$3.00
Elephants	$3.00

Plate 84. Left to right.

Plastic & steel, religious motto, M-Cor, U.S.A. $3.00
Plastic & steel, Jesus Is Lord, made in Hong Kong $3.00
Wood & steel, gold stamp praying hands, stainless, Hong Kong $3.00
Wood, plastic & steel, dual function, ruler & opener, Christ the Rule of Life, stainless steel,
    Japan $5.00
Plastic, Latin inscription $3.00
Pot metal & steel, Thanksgiving, made by Napier $8.00
Plastic, Sacred Heart Monastery, Hales Corners, Wisconsin $3.00
Plastic & steel, cross $3.00

Plate 85. Left to right.

Bust of Hawaiian greeter, foil sticker, Hawaiian Greeting, Poly-Art, LTD. $5.00
Hawaiian totem $4.00
Hawaiian hula girl $6.00
Hawaiian carved log $4.00
Hawaiian carved in fake pumice $4.00
Egyptian head, made in U.S.A. $5.00
Totem, Hawaii $5.00
King Kamehameha, made in Hawaii $6.00

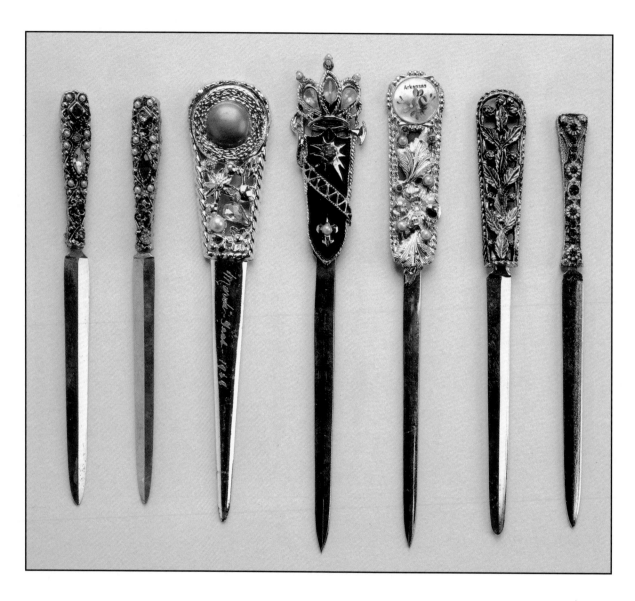

Plate 86. Left to right.

Gold plated, jeweled handle $8.00
Gold plated, jeweled handle $8.00
Silver plated, jeweled handle $7.00
Silver plated, crown, sun & fleur de lis $15.00
Gold plated, mother of pearl, Arkansas $8.00
Gold plated, floral handle $6.00
Gold plated, jeweled handle $8.00

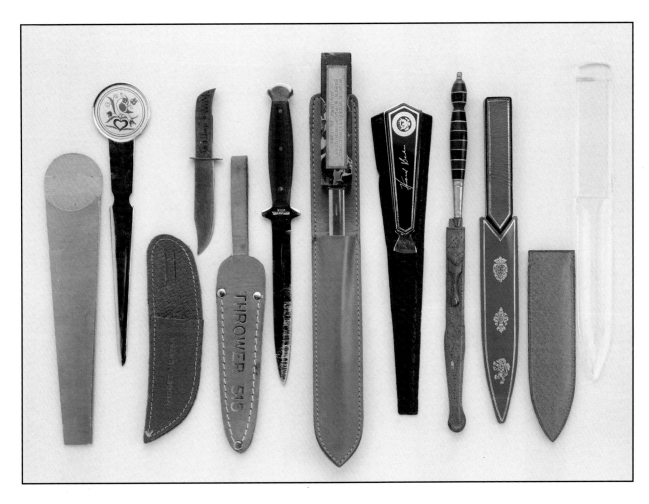

Plate 87. Left to right.

LEATHER

Brass & plastic, paper sheath, bird & heart $3.00
Wood & copper, Gallop, M. M. Midget Hunter on sheath $10.00
Exotic wood & steel, Thrower 515 on sheath, stainless steel, Japan $9.00
Marble & brass, World's Safety Record, Paper & Pulp Industry, January 15, 1959, made in
    Germany $15.00
Plastic & steel, Howard Baker, U. S. Senate $15.00
Bakelite, nickel & steel $45.00
Plastic & leather $3.00
Plastic magnifying blade $3.00

Plate 88. Left to right.

MISCELLANEOUS

Brass opener, plastic sheath, early American eagle motif, made in India $12.00
Leather & steel, stamped design in leather $10.00
Brass, key, Korea $20.00
Gold plated, plastic & steel opener, brass & leather sheath, Toledo design, Spain $15.00
Ground leather & steel, made in England $10.00

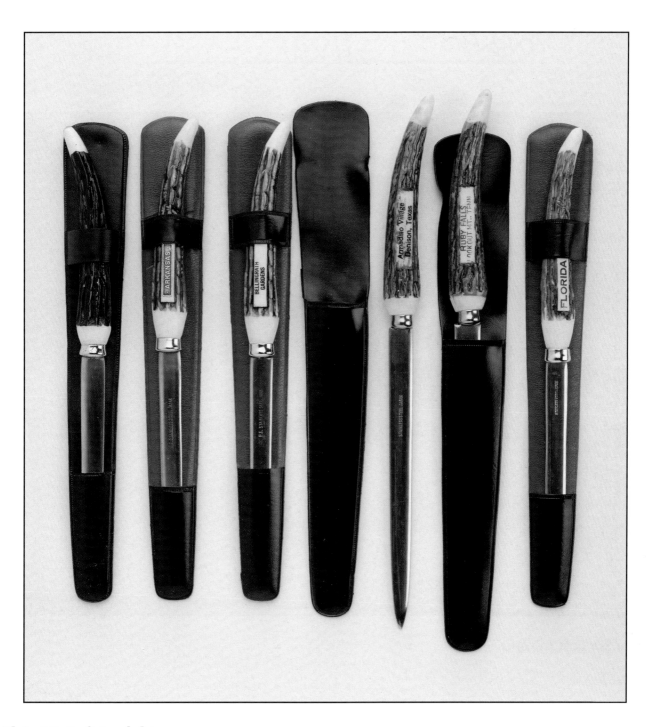

Plate 89. Left to right.

PLASTIC

Stainless steel, Japan $5.00
P.C. stainless steel, Arkansas, Japan $5.00
P.C. stainless steel, Bellingrath Gardens, Japan $5.00
P.C. stainless steel, Armadillo Village, Denison, Texas, Japan $5.00
Stainless steel, Ruby Falls, Lookout Mtn., Tenn., Japan $5.00
Stainless steel, Florida, Japan $5.00

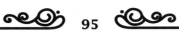

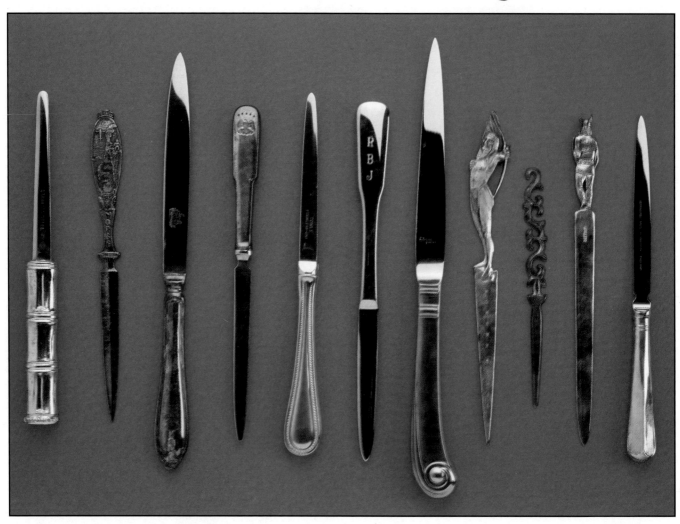

Plate 90. Left to right.

SILVER PLATED

Bamboo style handle $10.00
Map of Norway with plane & Norwegian boat, marked Norge on reverse, Hellic Olan &
    his shield, made by T.K. GOGP $65.00
Galleon etched on blade, handle marked Ex PR.NS. ALP $12.00
Continental eagle & stars, marked Gorham Stainless $15.00
Marked Towle Stainless $10.00
Monogramed handle, made in Japan $10.00
Marked Bridalan, Japan $12.00
Mohawk Trail, Mohawk chief with bow $75.00
Scrollwork handle $10.00
Viking, Norway, T.H. Marthinsen E.P.N.S., Norway $35.00
Made in Sheifield, England $12.00

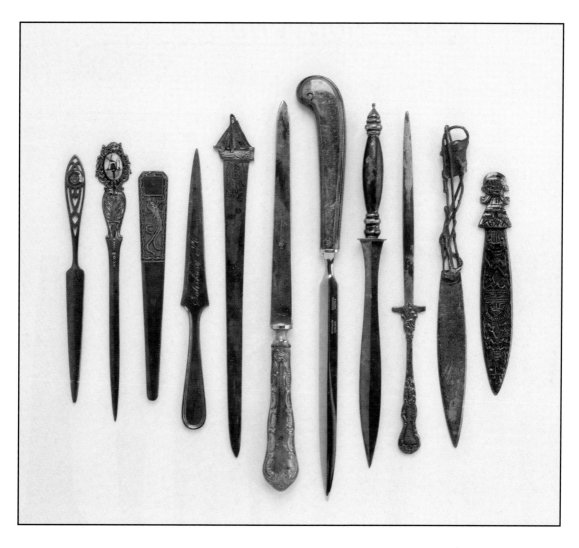

Plate 91. Left to right.

STERLING & SILVER

Pennsylvania State College, Hawks Sterling $15.00
Delft plaque, ALO Sterling $20.00
Peruvian bird, ATEMA 900 Silver $20.00
Salsbury, N.C., S. Kirk & Sons Sterling $20.00
Sailboat, N2 Lion Passant, Holland $25.00
Quebec, Birks Sterling $20.00
Sterling handle, Webster Sterling $15.00
Siam dancing god $45.00
Waring eagle landing on the British Crest, Sterling $40.00
Flag furled, marked 925 . . . .$50.00
Peru motif, Peru 925 . . . .$25.00

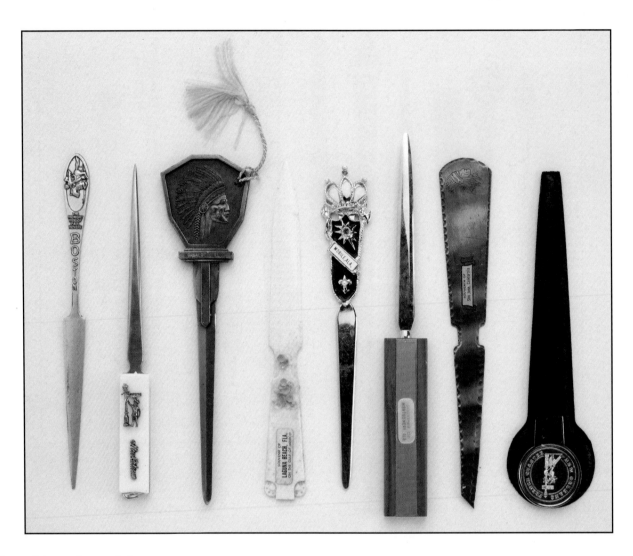

Plate 92. Left to right.

CITIES

Silver plate, Boston, The Midnight Ride of Paul Revere $10.00
Plastic & steel, New Orleans $8.00
Copper colored, Charlotte, N.C., Indian chief's head $8.00
Plastic with glued on shells, Laguna Beach, Fla. $4.00
Rhinestone, pot metal, steel, crown, Mobile, Ala. $10.00
Wood & steel, Montgomery, Ala. $4.00
Hammered copper, San Jose, California, Indian chief's head $10.00
Plastic & steel, plastic sheath, New Orleans French Quarter $4.00

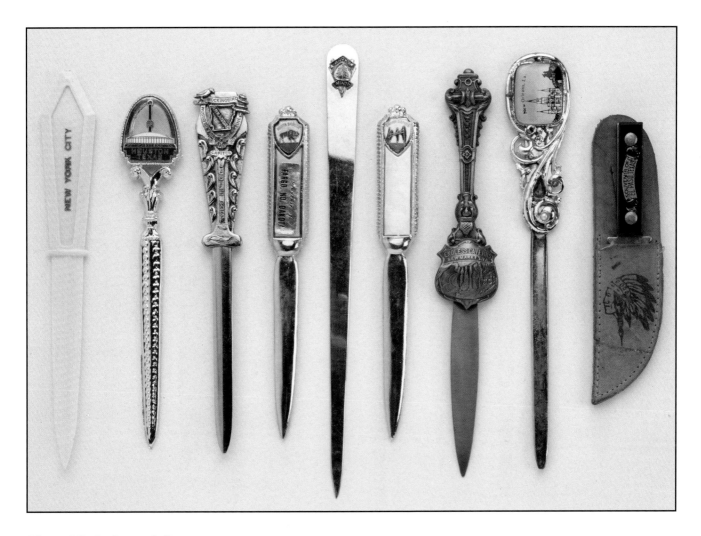

Plate 93. Left to right.

CITIES

Plastic, New York City, Cascade U.S.A. $3.00
Enamel, brass & pot metal, Houston, Texas, marked Fort $4.00
Pot metal & steel, Little Rock, Arkansas, marked Gish $5.00
Pot metal & plastic, Fargo, No. Dakota. $3.00
Pot metal & steel, Anoka, Minn. $10.00
Pot metal & plastic, Grand Rapids, Mich. $3.00
Bronze, Endless Caverns, New Market, Va. $8.00
Plastic, rhinestones, pot metal & steel, New Orleans, La., marked Jula $4.00
Bakelite & steel with leather sheath, El Paso, Texas, has Indian chief on sheath $15.00

Plate 94. Left to right.

CITIES

Silver plate, Natchez, Miss., Rosalie $8.00
Brass & steel, Spokane, Washington $4.00
Brass & steel, Eureka Springs, Arkansas, marked Union Japan $6.00
Gold plated, Denver $4.00
Reverse painted glass & steel, New York City $12.00
Brass & steel, Lexington, Kentucky $5.00
Silver plate, Nashville, Tenn., Andrew Jackson $8.00
Steel, plastic & pot metal, Park Rapids, Minn., logging camp $3.00
Plastic & steel, Las Vegas, Nev. $3.00
Enameled brass & steel, Plains, Ga. $5.00
Gold plated, New Orleans $3.00
Copper, Fulton, Mo., Winston Churchill Memorial $8.00
Enamel & steel, Corpus Christi, Texas, ABC 92 . . . .$4.00

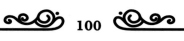

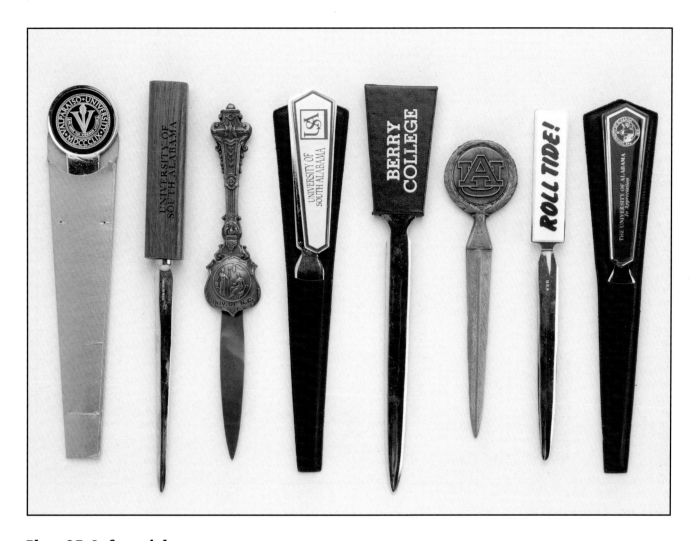

Plate 95. Left to right.

COLLEGES

Plastic & gold plate, paper sheath, Valparaiso University $3.00
Wood & gold plate, University of South Alabama, made in U.S.A. $3.00
Brass, University of N. C. $5.00
Plastic & steel, plastic sheath, University of South Alabama, made in U.S.A. $8.00
Leatherette & steel, Berry College $3.00
Brass colored, Auburn University $3.00
Plastic & steel, University of Alabama, Roll Tide, made in U.S.A. $4.00
Plastic & gold plate, plastic sheath, University of Alabama in Appreciation $3.00

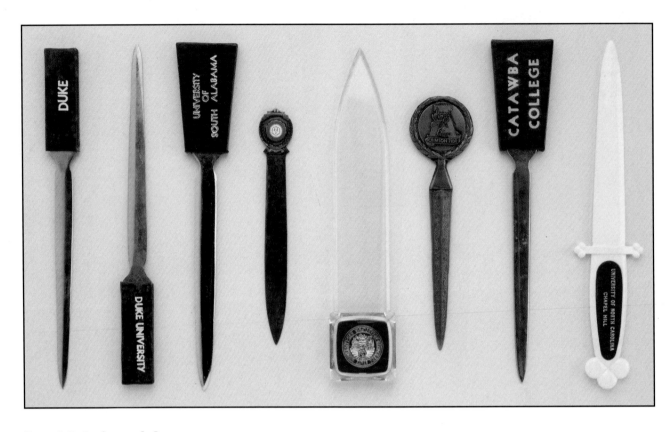

Plate 96. Left to right.

COLLEGES

Leatherette, gold plate, Duke $3.00
Leatherette, gold plate, Duke University $3.00
Leatherette & steel, University of South Alabama $3.00
Enamel & silver plate, University of Connecticut, 1881, made in Holland $15.00
Plastic, Henderson State University Arkadelphia, Ark. $3.00
Brass colored, University of Alabama Crimson Tide $4.00
Leatherette & goldplate, Catawba College $4.00
Leatherette & plastic, University of North Carolina, Chapel Hill $3.00

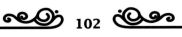

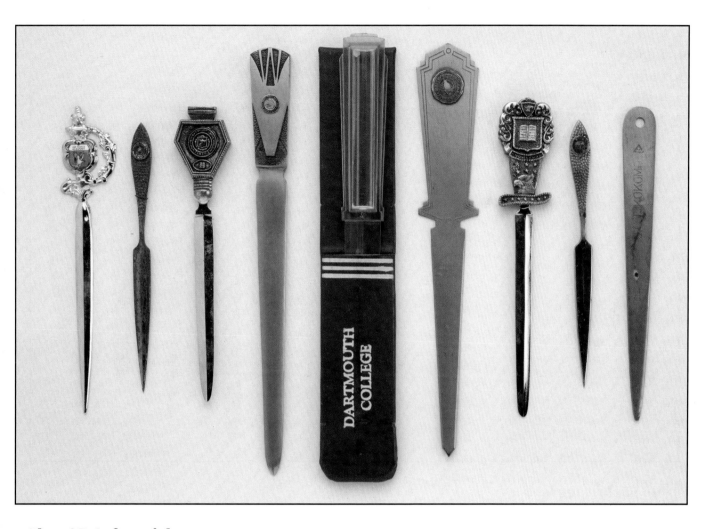

Plate 97. Left to right.

Colleges

Enamel & steel, Air Force Academy $5.00
Bronze & enamel, George Peabody College for Teachers $12.00
Pot metal & steel, University of Michigan $4.00
Bronze, Gustavus Adolphus Col., St. Peter, Minn. $12.00
Plastic & paper, dual purpose, magnifying handle, Dartmouth College, Sterling, U.S.A. $4.00
Brass, Syracuse University, marked Metal Arts Co., Rochester, N.Y. $6.00
Pot metal & steel, East Carolina $4.00
Copper plated, Clemson, A & M College $12.00
Diragold alloy, UTC KOKOMO $10.00

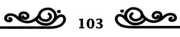

Plate 98. Left to right.

COUNTRIES

Silver plate, Radhusit, Oslo, Norway, marked Plett $20.00
Silver plated & enamel, London, The Old Curiosity Shop $15.00
Silver plated & enamel, Swiss Cross, marked Meka, Denmark $15.00
Silver content alloy, Equador $20.00
Brass & horn, Thailand $12.00
Steel, Ahus $6.00
Pewter & steel, Norway, marked H.S. Tinn $12.00
Brass & wood, made in Siam $15.00
Silver plated, Denmark $20.00
Silver plated, Pella Iowa $6.00
Brass, Mora $3.00

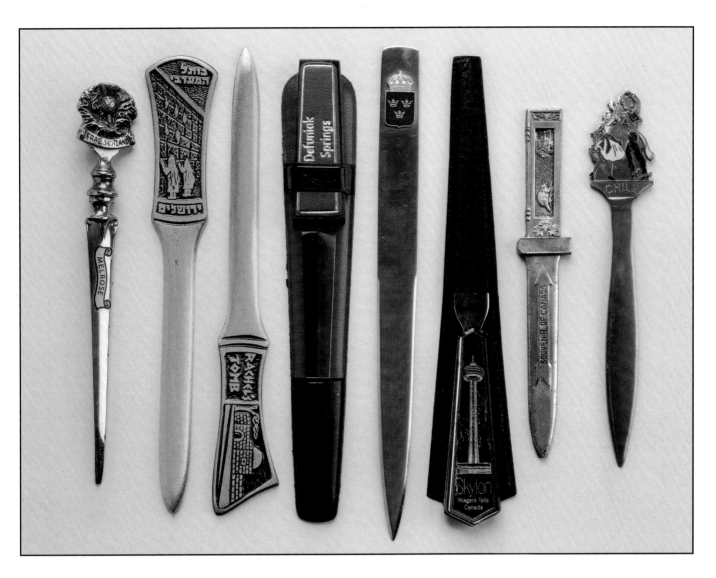

Plate 99. Left to right.

COUNTRIES

Gold-plated brass, Melrose, Scotland $10.00
Brass, The Wailing Wall made in Israel KL 892 . . . .$6.00
Brass, Rachel's Tomb, made in Israel, KL891 . . . .$6.00
Leathertte, wood & steel in plastic sheath, Dejuniak Springs, stainless steel Japan $4.00
Gold plate, enamel & steel, Sweden $10.00
Gold plate & plastic, plastic sheath, Niagara Falls, Canada $4.00
Silver plated, Canada, marked with helmed crest, registered $15.00
Enamel on copper, Chile, marked Ind. Chilena $12.00

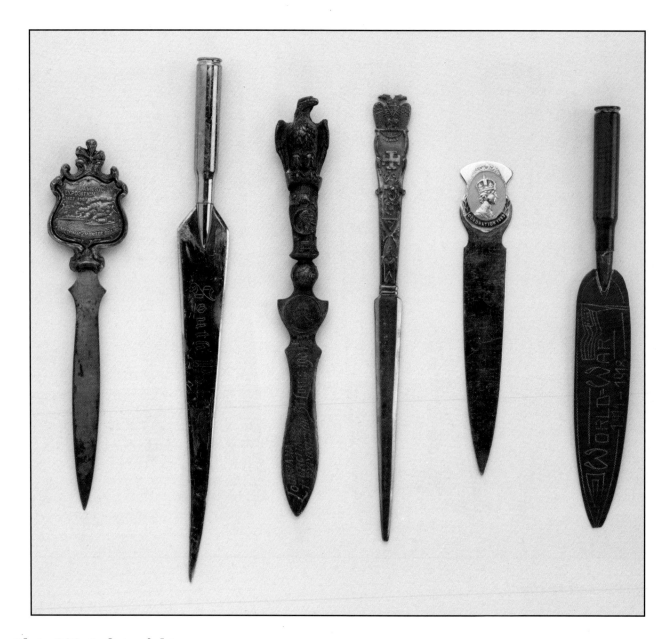

Plate 100. Left to right.

HISTORICAL EVENTS

Blade engraved St. Mihiel, white metal & silver plate, 1907 Jamestown Exposition,
    depicting Duel of the Merrymac & Moniter, very desirable $85.00
Brass, WWII cartridge, Trench Art, South Pacific, ca 1942 . . . .$25.00
Bronze, Louisiana Purchase Exposition, St. Louis World's Fair 1904, marked patented
    July 28, 1901, very desirable $125.00
Bronze, Mason Scottish Rites, Seattle $35.00
Silver plate & enamel, Queen Elizabeth's coronation 1953, marked Exquisite plate, made
    in England $25.00
Bronze, WWI brass cartridge, blade engraved World War with U.S. flag flying left
    1914–1918, reverse side, German prisoner, very desirable $85.00

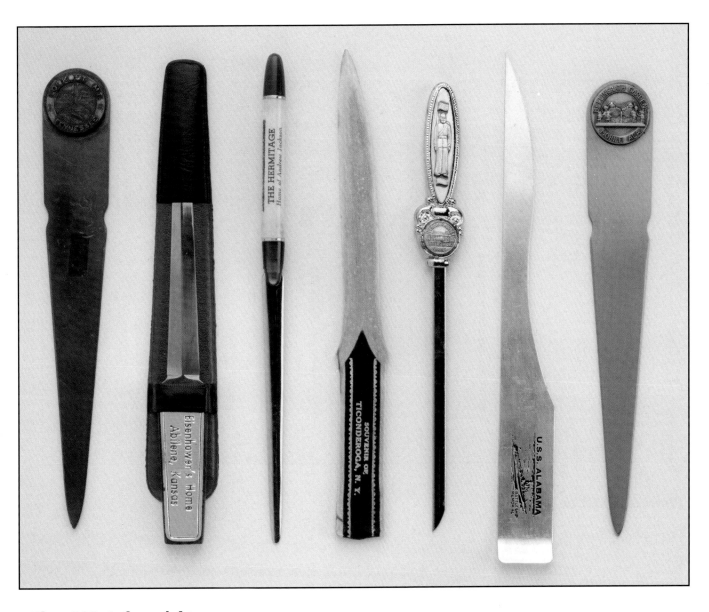

Plate 101. Left to right.

HISTORICAL PLACES

Copper, Lookout Mountain, Tennessee $10.00
Leather, wood & steel with plastic sheath, Eisenhower's home, Abilene, Kansas $5.00
Plastic, celluloid & gold plate, bullet pistol handle, The Hermitage, Home of Andrew Jackson .$6.00
Leather & plastic, Ticonderoga, N.Y. $3.00
Silver plate, pot metal & steel, Beauvoir House, Jefferson Davis Shrine $8.00
Aluminum, U.S.S. Alabama Battleship Memorial $8.00
Copper, Bellingrath Gardens, Mobile, Ala. $6.00

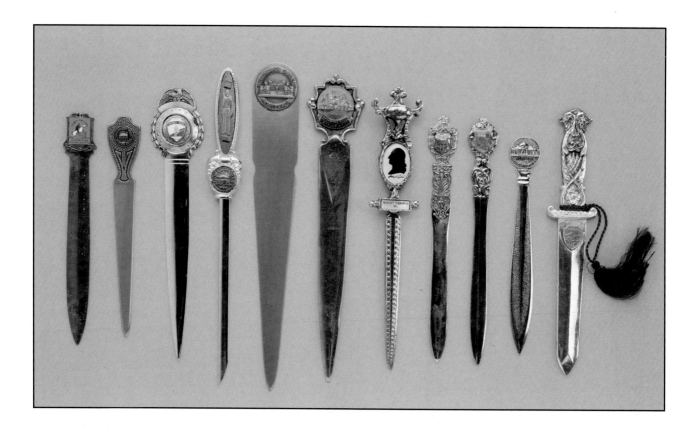

Plate 102. Left to right.

HISTORICAL PLACES

Silver plated, Wiggins Old Tavern 1786 North Hampton, Massachusetts, made in Holland . . .$15.00
Bronze, Paul Revere House, Boston, Mass. $6.00
Enamel & steel, Chimney Rock, N.C. $6.00
Gold plated, Beauvoir House, Jefferson Davis Shrine $8.00
Copper, Bellingrath Gardens, Mobile, Ala. $6.00
Brass & enamel, Sagamore Hills, Oyster Bay, marked Peerage England $25.00
Pot metal & plastic, silhouette of George Washington, Mt. Vernon, Va. $12.00
Enamel & steel, Mark Twain, Hannibal Mo., marked Kelpa Arts $10.00
Silver plated, Polynesian Cultural Center, Oahu $15.00
White metal, Monticello & Charlottsville, Va., made in Holland $6.00
White metal & brass, Blowing Rock, N.C. $8.00

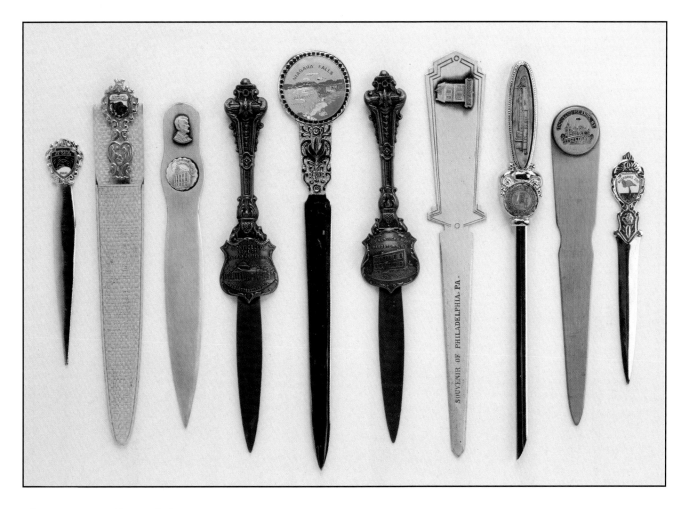

Plate 103. Left to right.

HISTORICAL PLACES

White metal & enamel, Shoshone Ice Caves, Idaho $4.00
White metal, plastic sheath, Stamping Ground, Ky. $4.00
Steel, Lincoln Museum, Washington D.C. $6.00
Brass, Monticello, home of Thomas Jefferson, Charlottesville, Va. $15.00
Plastic & steel, Niagara Falls, made in Japan $4.00
Brass, Old Kentucky Home, Bardstown, Ky. $15.00
White metal, Betsy Ross house, Philadelphia, Pa., marked Metal Arts Co., Rochester, NY $15.00
White metal, Audubon Memorial, St. Francisville, La. $10.00
Brass, Boldt Castle, Alexandria Bay, Thousand Island, NY $8.00
White metal, Columbia, S.C. $4.00

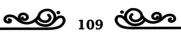

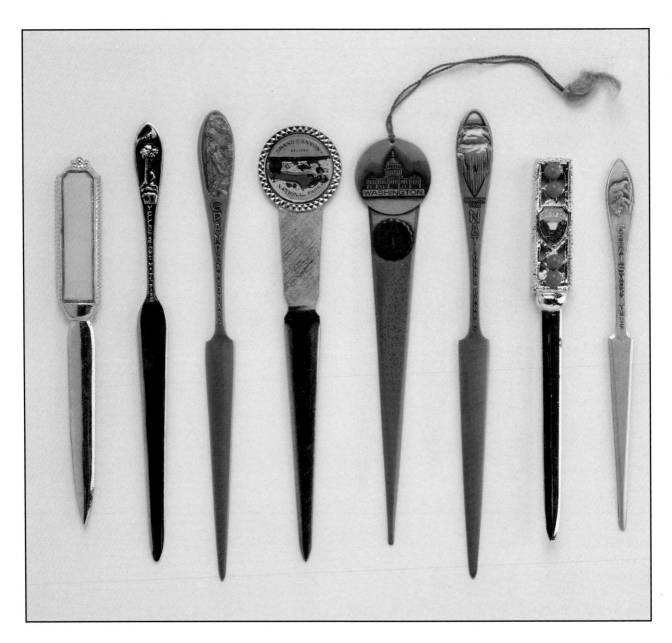

Plate 104. Left to right.

NATIONAL PARKS

Gold plated & plastic, Great Smoky Mtns. $3.00
White metal, Old Faithful, Yellowstone $4.00
Bronze, Grand Canyon, Ariz. $7.00
Plastic & gold plate, Grand Canyon $4.00
Copper, Washington $7.00
Copper, Mammoth Cave, Ky. $8.00
White metal & plastic, Hoover Dam, Nev. $4.00
Silver washed, Great Smoky Mts. $6.00

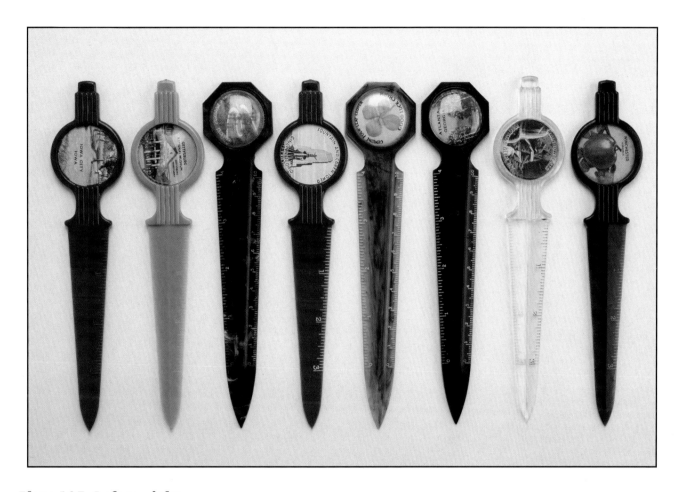

Plate 105. Left to right.

PLASTIC — RULERS

Iowa City, Iowa $4.00
Gettysburg National Museum $4.00
The Loop, Great Smoky Mts. $4.00
Fountain & Carew Tower, Cincinnati, Ohio $4.00
On Front, Genuine four-leaf clover, on back John W. Roggie, Cathage, NY (dairy farm) $15.00
Atlanta, Georgia $4.00
Rainbow Falls, Watkins Glen, N.Y. $4.00
Winchester, Virginia $4.00

Plate 106. Left to right.

SCENIC — WOOD

Hand-painted flowers $20.00
Hand-painted scene, Venezuela $15.00
Hand-carved, painted alligator, Jacksonville, Fla. $35.00
Hand painted, El Salvador, C.A. $10.00
Hand painted, Asheville, N.C. $15.00
Hand painted, country home $10.00

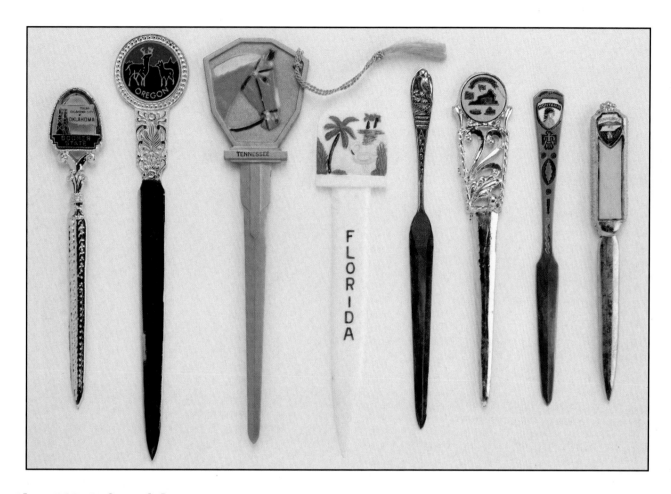

Plate 107. Left to right.

STATES

Gold plated, Oklahoma, marked Fort $6.00
Steel, Oregon $6.00
Painted metal, Tennessee $12.00
Plastic, Florida $5.00
Gold plated, Alabama $4.00
Gold plated, Virginia $4.00
Copper, Montana $6.00
Gold plate & plastic, Tennessee $3.00

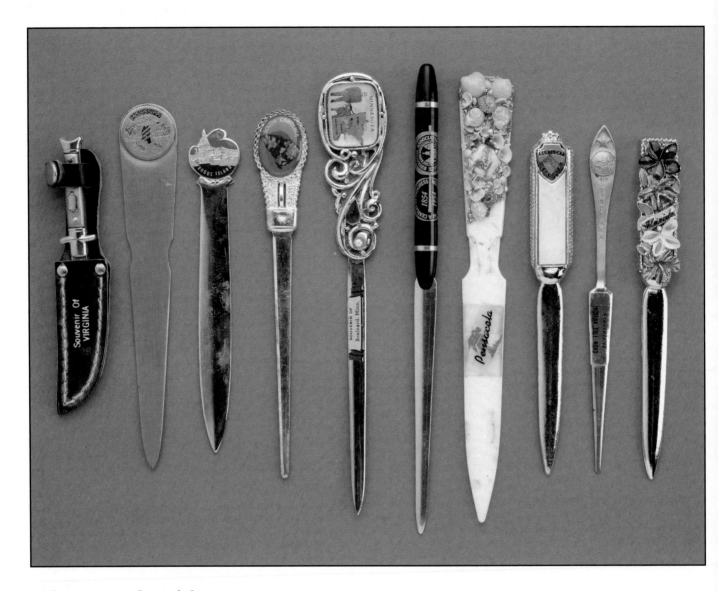

Plate 108. Left to right.

STATES

Plastic & steel with leather sheath, blade marked Colonial Prov., R.I. USA Virginia $6.00
Brass, Mississippi $4.00
Enamel & white metal, Rhode Island $6.00
Plastic, white metal, South Carolina $4.00
Plastic, gold plated with rhinestones, Minnesota $6.00
Plastic, bullet handle, gold plate, Iowa State Education Assoc. $5.00
Plastic with seashells on handle Pensacola Florida $3.00
Enamel, plastic & gold plate, Kentucky $3.00
Silver plated, Indiana Souvenir of Indiana Toll Road $10.00
Painted pot metal, Florida $3.00

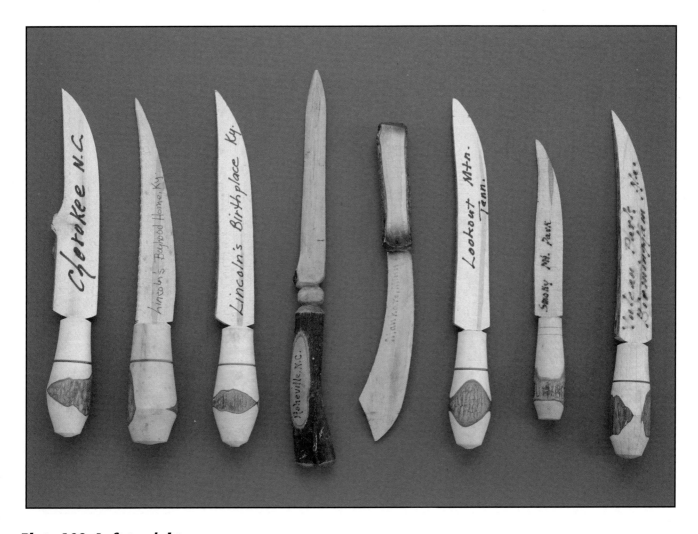

Plate 109. Left to right.

WOOD DAGGERS

Cherokee, N.C. $5.00
Lincoln's boyhood home; Ky. $5.00
Lincoln's birthplace, Ky. $5.00
Asheville, N.C. $10.00
Mankata, Minn. $5.00
Lookout Mt., Tenn. $5.00
Smoky Mt. Park $5.00
Vulcan Park, Birmingham, Ala. $5.00

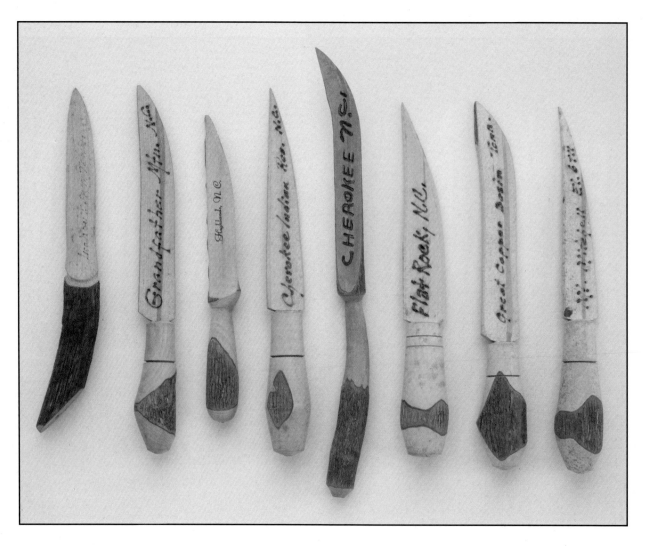

Plate 110. Left to right.

WOOD DAGGERS

Lookout Mt., Tenn. $5.00
Grandfather Mtn., N.C. $5.00
Highlands, N.C. $5.00
Cherokee Indian Res., N.C. $5.00
Cherokee, N.C. $5.00
Flat Rock, N.C. $5.00
Great Copper Basin, Tenn. $5.00
Mt. Mitchell, El 6711 . . . .$5.00

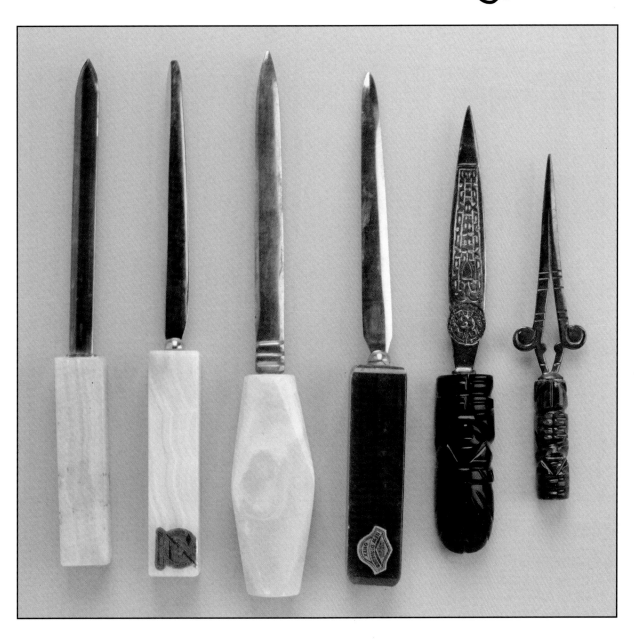

Plate 111. Left to right.

Onyx & brass, Penn. Turnpike, marked Germany $10.00
Onyx & gold plate $10.00
Onyx & brass $12.00
Dyed onyx & steel $10.00
Black onyx & sterling, Peruvian motif $45.00
Green onyx & sterling, Latin American motif $35.00

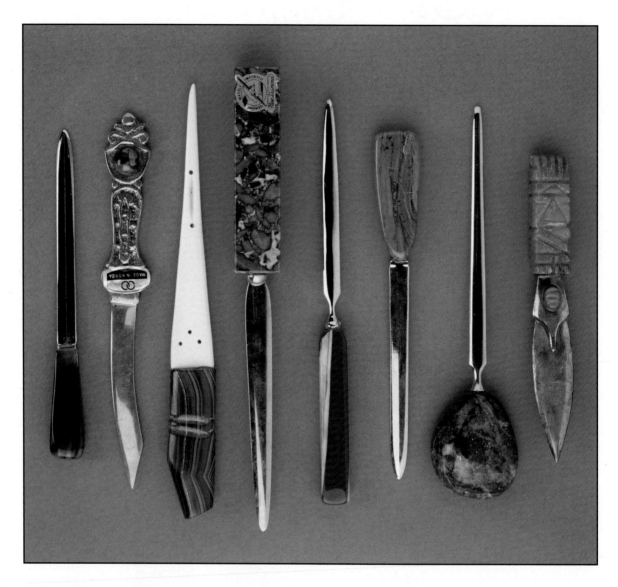

Plate 112. Left to right.

Agate & white metal $8.00
Brass with jasper stone $10.00
Ivory & malachite $70.00
Marble & gold plate $12.00
Dyed agate & steel $10.00
Agate & steel $12.00
Pyrite in jasper matrix & steel $15.00
Green onyx & sterling, made in Mexico $45.00

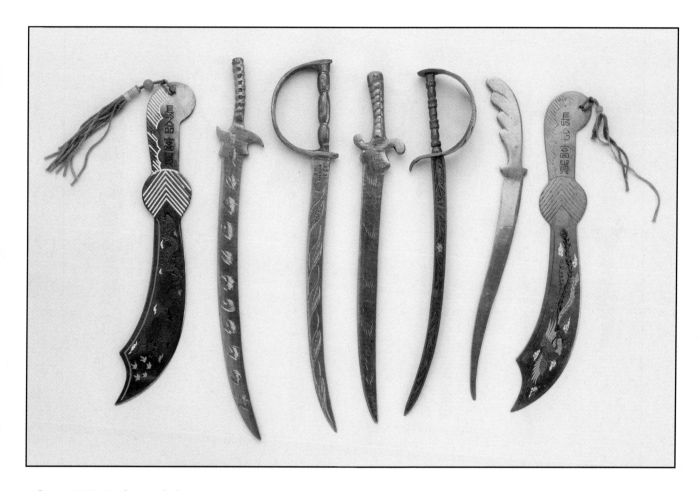

Plate 113. Left to right.

BRASS

Dragon motif, marked Taiwan $12.00
Engraved blade, marked JEE India $8.00
Engraved blade, marked NYK India 1650x $8.00
Engraved blade $6.00
Floral design, marked India 451F $10.00
Feather hilt $8.00
Dragon motif, made in Taiwan $12.00

Plate 114. Left to right.

COPPER

Vermont	.$5.00
Utah	.$4.00
Mitchell, N.C.	.$5.00
Mobile, Ala., made in Japan	.$5.00
Lebanon, Ky.	.$5.00
Griffin's head, Tampa, Fla.	.$10.00
Piece of eight motif	.$12.00

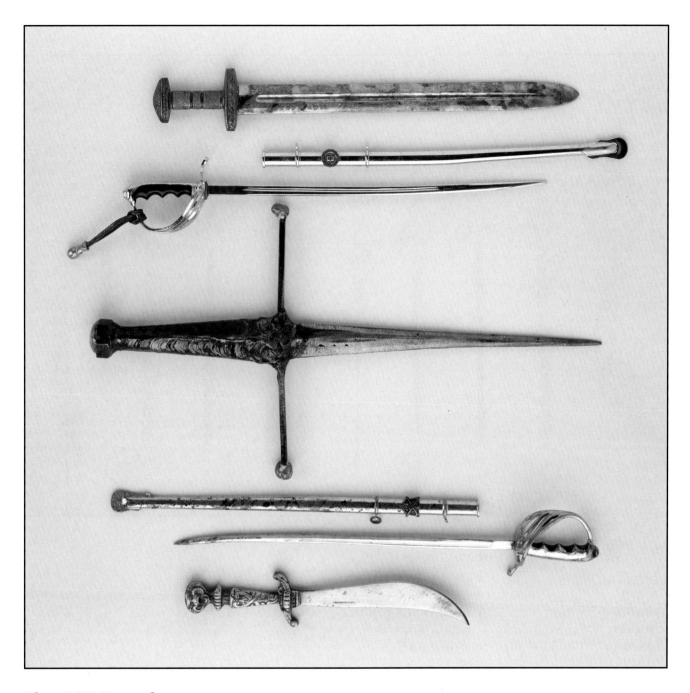

Plate 115. Top to bottom.

MISCELLANEOUS

Brass & silver plate, stamped The Viking Sword, Norway $25.00
Steel with boullion tassle, Indiana University $15.00
Cast-iron & brass, heavy dagger $8.00
Silver plated brass, American eagle with crossed swords on shield $12.00
Nickel, stamped Montagnmnmi, Italy $12.00

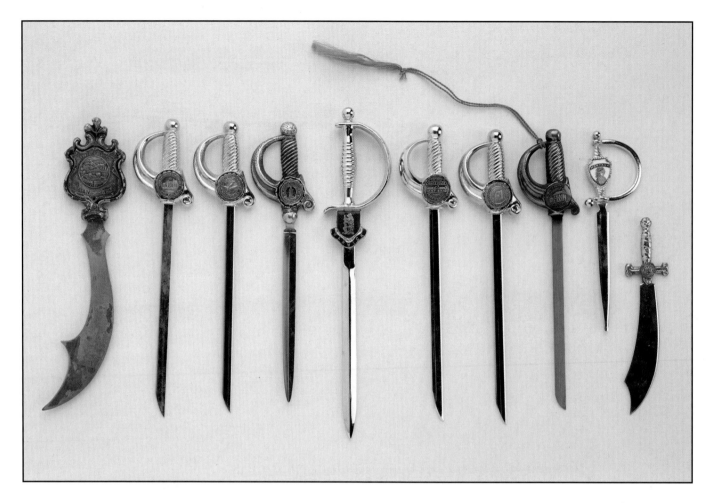

Plate 116. Left to right.

MISCELLANEOUS

Silver plate, Art Nouveau, State of Ohio Miamisburg $30.00
Gold color metal, Home of Franklin D. Roosevelt, Hyde Park, N.Y. $6.00
White metal, Municipal Airport, Atlanta, Ga. $7.00
White metal, Luther College $5.00
White metal & enamel, Warwick, made in England $8.00
Gold color metal, the little White House $9.00
White metal, the birthplace of Andrew Johnson, Raleigh, N.C. $7.00
Copper color, Washington's headquarters, Valley Forge, Pa. $7.00
Gold plate, Montana $4.00
Gold plated & steel, MIT $4.00

Plate 117. Left to right.

MISCELLANEOUS

Brass, made in Korea $10.00
Bronze & enamel, Royal Crest of Denmark, marked ARGENIUS Bronze, Denmark II $30.00
Gold color metal, Souvenir of Pittsburg, Pa., Block House 1764 . . . .$8.00
Two cast-iron cutlasses, ea $3.00
Brass $12.00

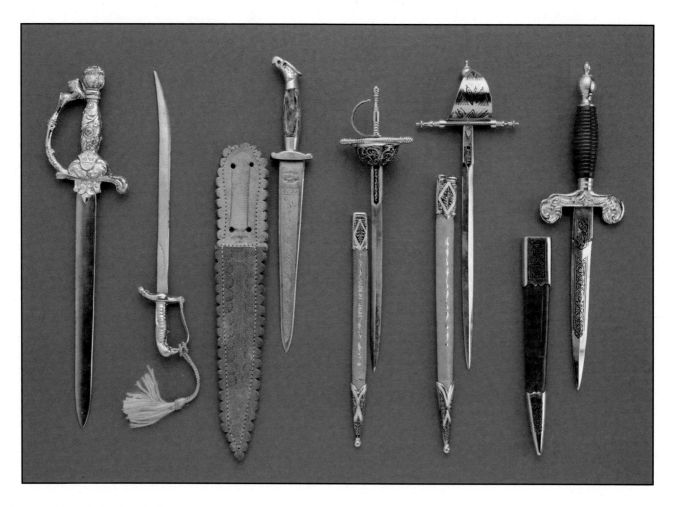

Plate 118. Left to right.

MISCELLANEOUS

White metal & steel, serated edge on blade $10.00
White metal, Lincoln's birthplace, KY $12.00
White metal & plastic, eagle head with etched blade, Mexican motif & leather sheath, made in
  Mexico $18.00
Toledo work, with leather sheath & Toledo tip, made in Spain $20.00
Toledo work, with leather sheath, marked Toledo on blade $20.00
Toledo work with plastic handle & leather sheath, marked Toledo $15.00

Plate 119. Left to right.

MISCELLANEOUS

Wood & Toledo Work $15.00
Toledo work with rhinestone handle $8.00
Toledo work with leather sheath, marked Toledo $35.00
Brass, enamel & mother of pearl, Oriental characters $18.00
Gold plate, enamel & steel, Monaco, marked DRAGO $18.00
Toledo work with rhinestone handle, marked Toledo, Spain $18.00
Toledo decorated brass, Spain $25.00

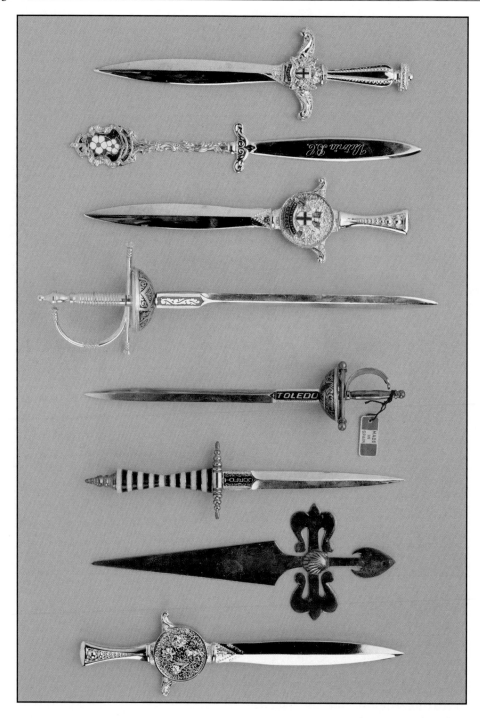

Plate 120. Top to bottom.

MISCELLANEOUS

White metal, London, made in England $8.00
White metal & enamel, Victoria, B.C. $10.00
White metal, Scottish motto & London $8.00
Toledo work, made in Spain $15.00
Toledo work, made in Spain, with original paper label $20.00
Brass & nylon, marked Toledo $10.00
Silver plate, seashell over cross $25.00
White metal, on reverse, enamel plaque showing bagpipe player, Scottish motto $15.00

Plate 121. Left to right.

MISCELLANEOUS

Gold plated, Birmingham, Ala. $5.00
Gold plated, sea horse and fish, Florida. $8.00
Gold plated, India $4.00
Toledo work with polyester handle, made in Spain $12.00
Toledo work with Spanish Royal Crest, marked Toledo, early piece $30.00
Gold plate, Ky. $4.00
Gold plate, Ashland, Lexington, Ky. $5.00
Brass, plain $5.00
Gold plated, Governor's Palace, Williamsburg, Vir. $5.00
Gold plate, Des Moines, Iowa $3.00

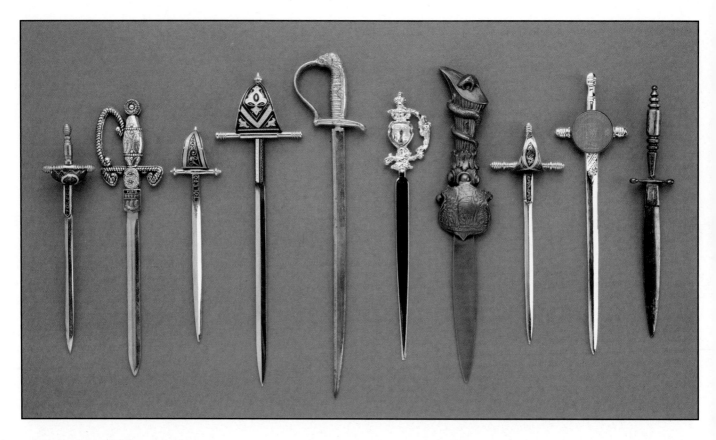

Plate 122. Left to right.

MISCELLANEOUS

Toledo work, Toledo, Spain $12.00
White metal, Paris, marked Depose $5.00
Damascene, marked Toledo $18.00
Damascene $22.00
Gold-plated handle $6.00
White metal, National Tower, Gettysburg, Pa. $5.00
Brass colored, Natural Bridge, Va. $15.00
Toledo work, marked Spain $10.00
Gold plated, Oklahoma $4.00
Silver, marked Silver $20.00

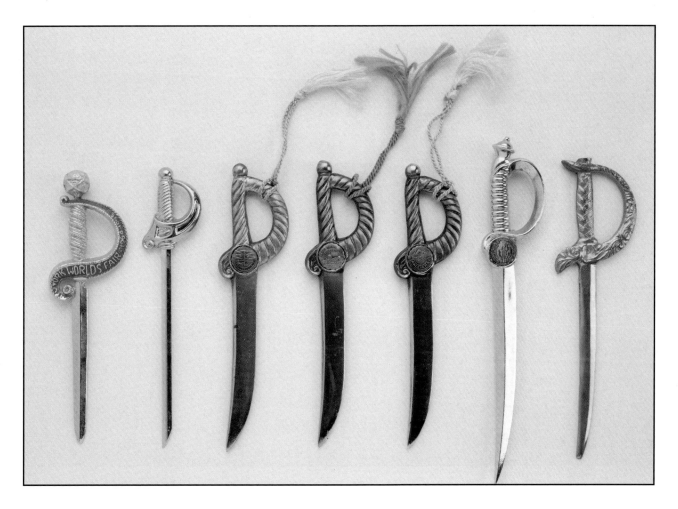

Plate 123. Left to right.

MISCELLANEOUS

Gold plated, New York World's Fair 1964–65 . . . .$10.00
Gold plated, Mobile, Ala. $5.00
Gold plated, Great Smoky Mts. $5.00
Gold plated, State Capitol, Jackson, Miss. $5.00
Gold plated, Raleigh, N.C. $5.00
Gold plated, Charlottesville, Va. $5.00
Brass $5.00

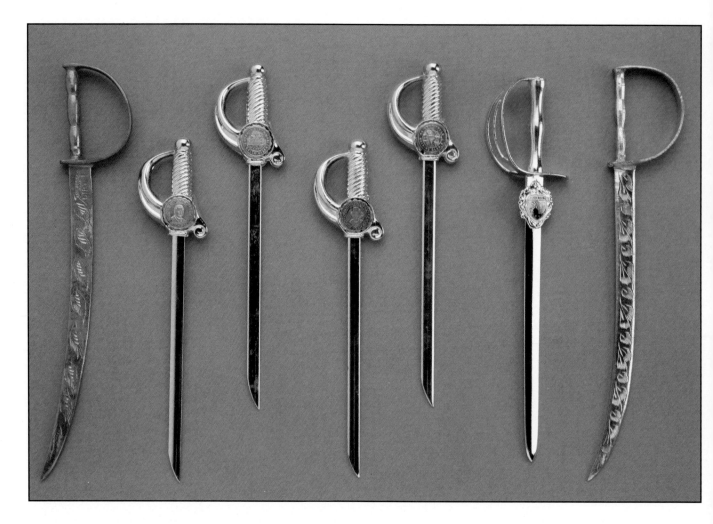

Plate 124. Left to right.

MISCELLANEOUS

Brass, engraved blade, marked SARNABRASS, India 5187-1 . . . .$10.00
Gold plated, Warren G. Harding, Marion, Ohio. $5.00
Gold plated, The House of Seven Gables, Salem, Mass. $5.00
Gold plated, The Pirates' House, Savannah, Ga. $5.00
Gold plated, Rainbow Falls, Watkins Glen, N.Y. $5.00
Gold plated & steel, Vereeniging $5.00
Brass, marked India $10.00

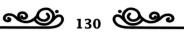

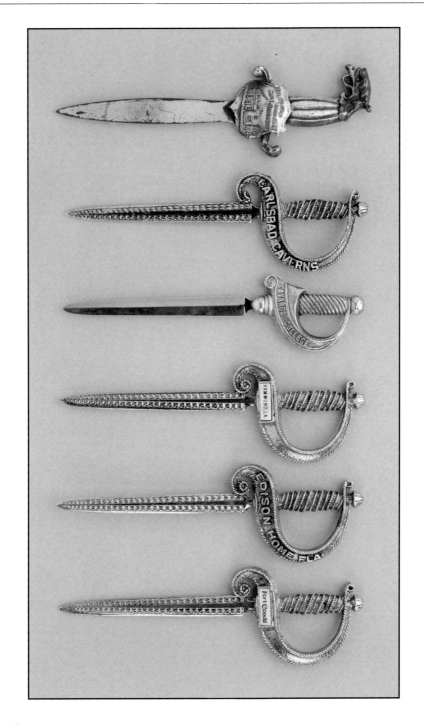

Plate 125. Top to bottom.

WHITE METAL

The Alamo, San Antonio $18.00
Carlsbad Caverns $5.00
Catawba College $5.00
Hammond, La. $5.00
Edison Home, Fla. $5.00
Fort. Condé $5.00

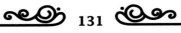

Plate 126. Left to right.

WOOD

Needlepoint look $15.00
Abalone inlay $15.00
Carved design, marked Yugoslovia $10.00
Pennsylvania Dutch carved design $18.00
Hand carved, marked Singet Po Stiklestad $10.00
Engraved & painted floral design $25.00
Marquetry work $18.00

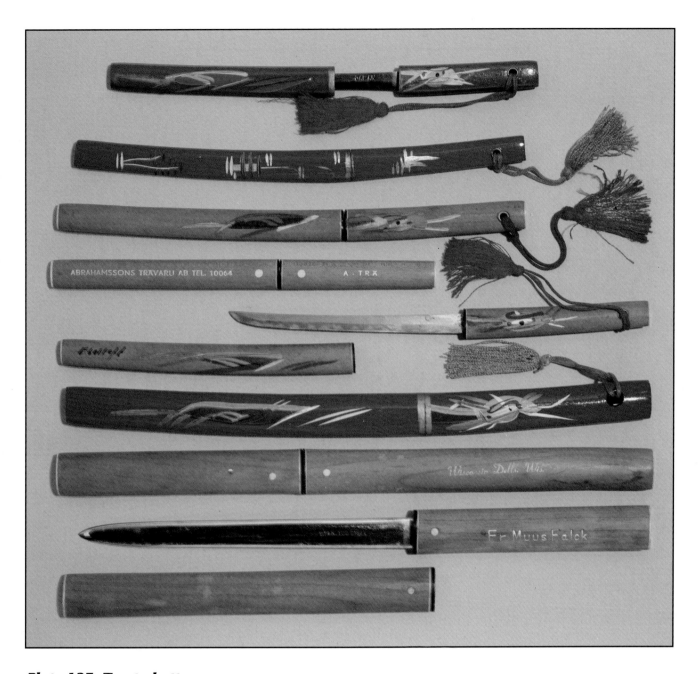

Plate 127. Top to bottom.

WOOD HANDLE & SHEATH

Japanese type swords used in Seppuku ceremony.

Marked Japan $10.00
Marked FIC Japan $10.00
Marked Japan $8.00
Abrahamsson's Travel $8.00
Ebeltoft, marked MCO $10.00
Marked Japan $12.00
Wisconsin Dells, Wis., marked P.C. Japan $8.00
Fr. Muus Falck $7.00

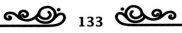

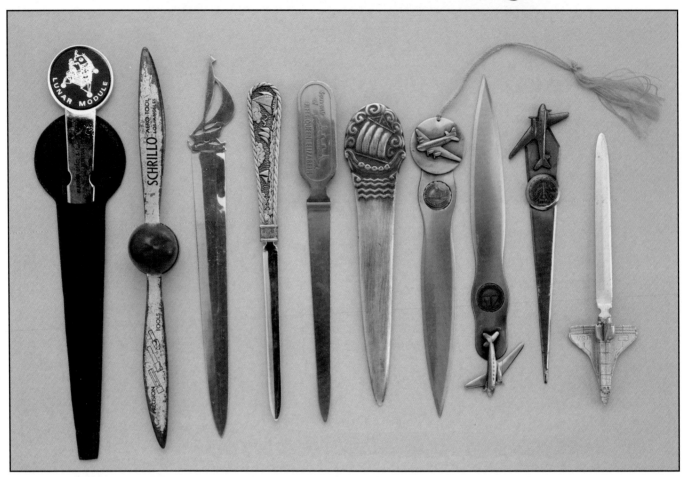

Plate 128. Left to right.

Plastic white metal with plastic sheath, LUNAR MODULE $10.00
Silver plate & brass, propellor shaped, Schrillo Aero Tools, Los Angeles, marked
    Pat. no. 2237461, St. Paul, U.S.A. $75.00
Brass, sailboat, marked Andarbat M.S. $10.00
Pewter, sailboats, marked Pewter Images $8.00
Copper, souvenir of RMS Queen Elizabeth $15.00
Pewter, Viking ship $7.00
Copper, airplane $15.00
Copper, airplane $15.00
Copper, airplane $15.00
White metal, Space Shuttle, marked Fort $15.00

Trowels

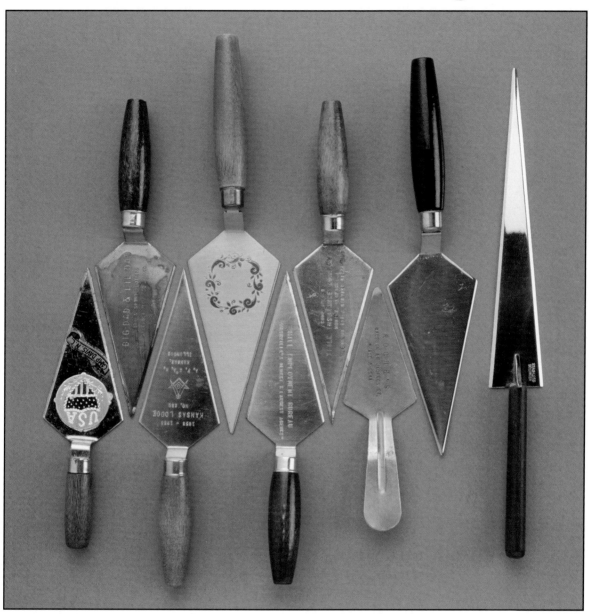

Plate 129. Left to right.

TROWELS

Aluminum & steel, Camp Davis, N. C.	$6.00
Brass, Big Dad & Lil Dad	$8.00
Brass, Kansas Lodge	$10.00
Brass, floral design	$6.00
Brass, Hill Employment Bureau	$6.00
Brass, Title Insurance Co.	$6.00
Brass, Roche's	$5.00
Brass, plain	$6.00
Stainless steel	$8.00

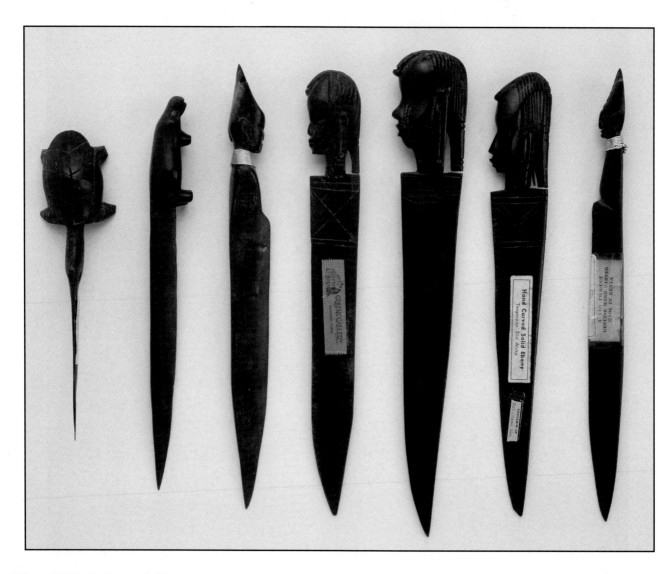

Plate 130. Left to right.

AFRICAN

Turtle $15.00
Hippopotomus $15.00
Native head $10.00
Native head $12.00
Native head $12.00
Native head $12.00
Native head $10.00

Plate 131. Top to bottom.

AFRICAN

Duck $20.00
Chicken $20.00
Native head $10.00
Native head $12.00
Totem $8.00

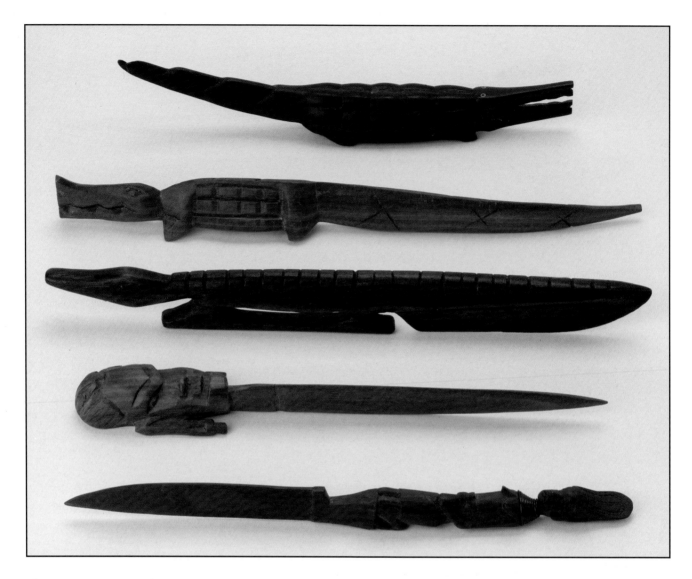

Plate 132. Top to bottom.

AFRICAN

Crocodile $16.00
Crocodile $12.00
Crocodile $12.00
Native head $10.00
Nude native woman $15.00

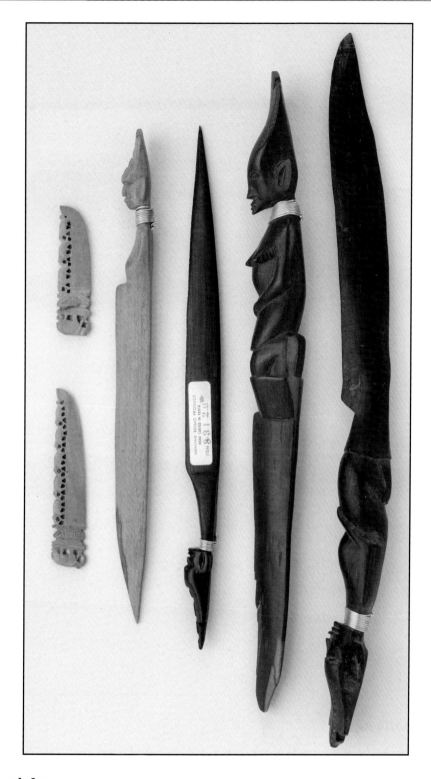

Plate 133. Left to right.

AFRICAN

Two small herds of elephants, ea. $6.00
Native head $8.00
Native head $8.00
Nude native woman $15.00
Nude native man $15.00

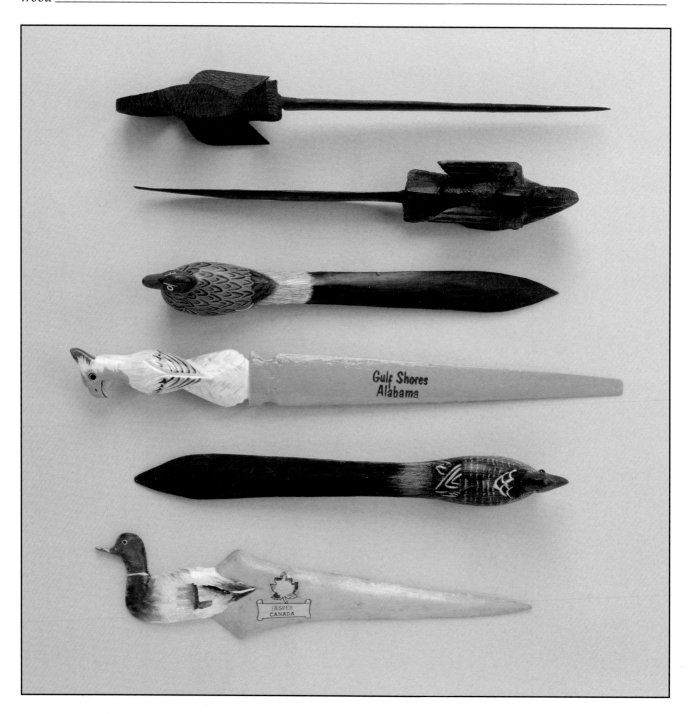

Plate 134. Top to bottom.

BIRDS

Goose $15.00
Duck $15.00
Duck, hand painted $8.00
Parrot, hand painted $10.00
Duck, hand painted $8.00
Duck, hand painted $10.00

Plate 135. Left to right.

CARVED

Bear cub $8.00
Owl, Ozark Foothills Guild, hand carved by Calvin Sloan $12.00
Leaves $15.00
Sea horse $10.00
Indian head $12.00
Horse head, hand carved by M. Brasher $15.00

Plate 136. Top to bottom.

CARVED

Fish, made in Yugoslavia $12.00
Nature god, Honduras C.A. $12.00
Grape motif $10.00
Abstract $8.00
Native god $6.00

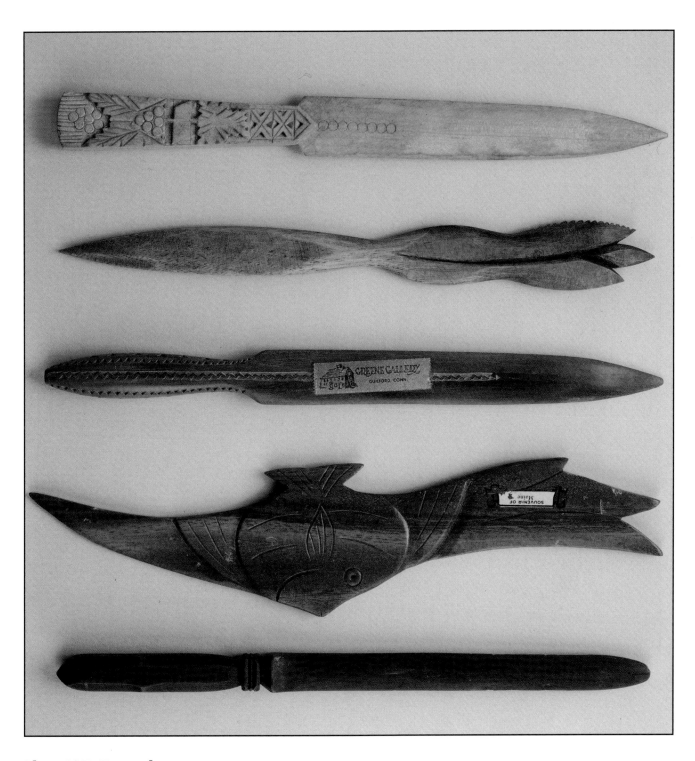

Plate 137. Top to bottom.

CARVED

Grape motif $6.00
Abstract $6.00
Abstract $8.00
Angel fish $15.00
Dagger $6.00

Plate 138. Left to right.

CARVED.

Sword, Souvenir of Union Station, St. Louis, Mo. $10.00
Squirrel, made by Berea College, Berea, Ky. $15.00
Cowboy boots, Dallas, Texas $10.00
Cowboy boot $12.00
Alligator, Biloxi, Miss. $18.00
Rifle $10.00

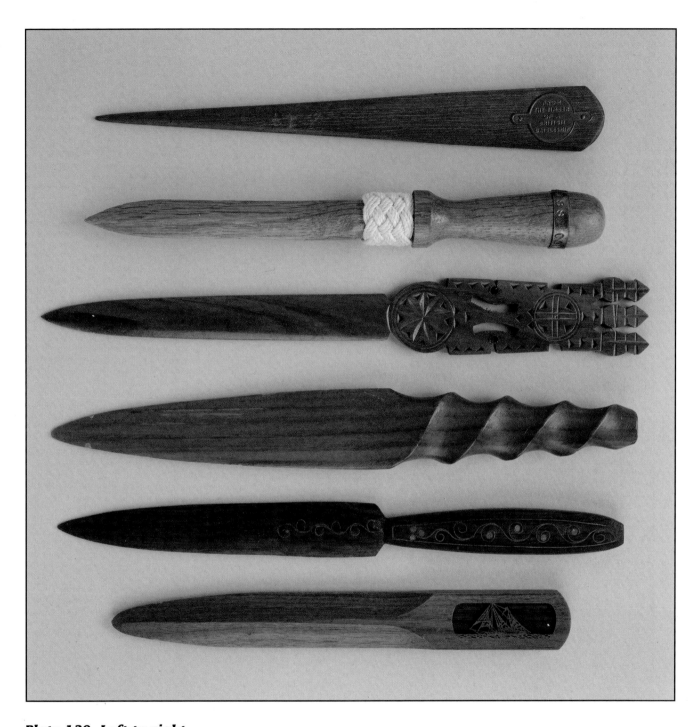

Plate 139. Left to right.

CARVED

Plain from timber of British battleship $6.00
Souvenior of U.S.S. Constitution $10.00
Castle $8.00
Abstract $6.00
Wire work, made by Sarna, India 62-791 . . . .$12.00
Sailboat, laser carved $8.00

Plate 140. Left to right.

CARVED

Birds, scratch painted $5.00
Jefferson Davis Shrine $8.00
Hilo, Hawaii $6.00
Plum handle dagger, signed Maihaugen $12.00
St. Paul, Minn. $6.00
Marquetry, ALSA Jerusalem $12.00

Plate 141. Left to right.

CARVED

Two abstract, Yugoslovia, ea. $6.00
Two with sea horse cutout, OMC Japan, ea. $8.00
Grape motif $8.00
Plain, made by League of Arts & Crafts of N.H. $6.00

Plate 142. left to right.

FIGURAL

Otter	$6.00
Native	$6.00
Native, Hawaii	$8.00
Rabbit, Berea College, Berea, Ky.	$15.00
Hawaiian figure, Honolulu	$15.00
Totem, KIA ORA Wellington, N.Z.	$25.00
Native	$6.00

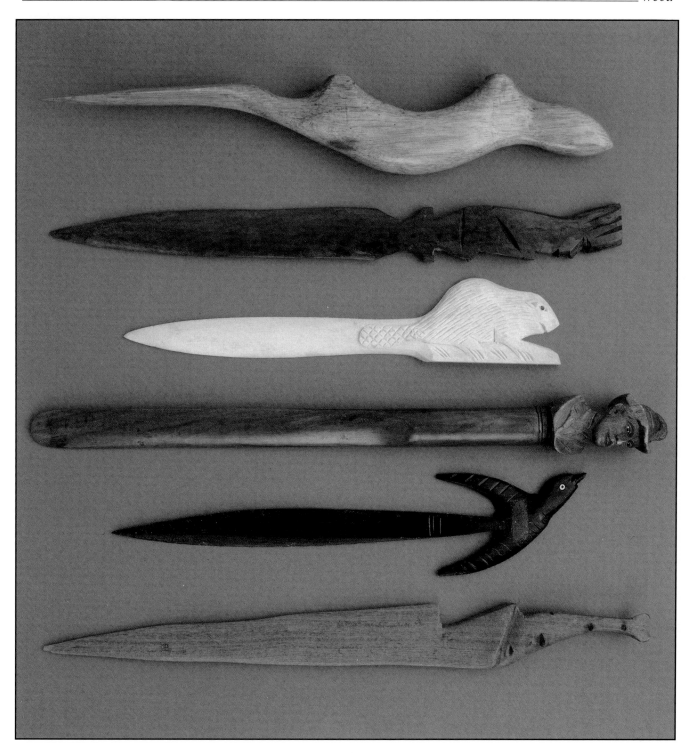

Plate 143. Top to bottom.

FIGURAL

Otter	$8.00
Native figure, Philippines	$6.00
Beaver	$15.00
English duke, with ivory eyes	$25.00
Swallow, Tanzania	$8.00
Giraffe	$8.00

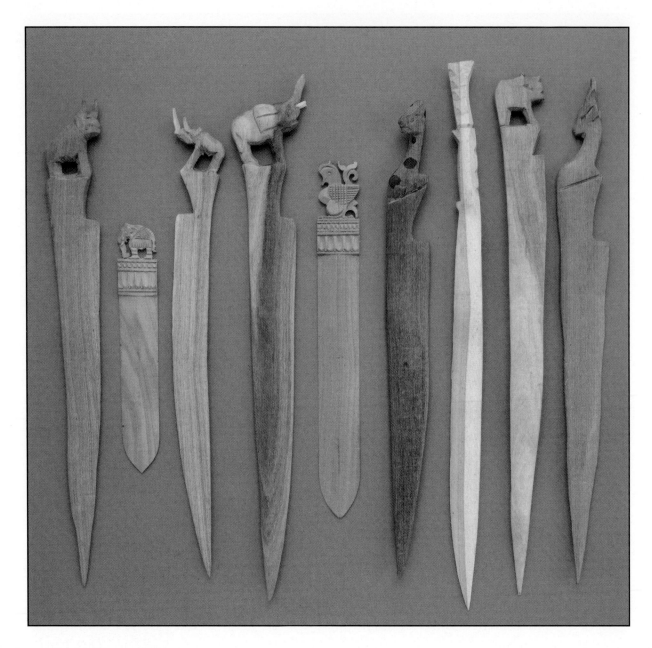

Plate 144. Left to right.

FIGURAL

Rhino $5.00
Elephant, India $5.00
Rhino, Kenya $5.00
Elephant with horn tusk $8.00
Stylized hen, India $8.00
Giraffe $7.00
Aardvark $5.00
Rhino, Kenya $5.00
Antelope, Kenya $5.00

Plate 145. Left to right.

MISCELLANEOUS

Twig sheath & handle, Minn., made in Japan $8.00
Turquoise, carnellian & opal $20.00
St. Peter, Minn. $6.00
Norris Dam TVA, Tenn. $4.00
Barney 1932 . . . .$4.00
Handmade in Bethlehem — Jordan $8.00
Abstract, marked Amy $6.00
Plain $6.00
Plain, Lord Cromwell England $8.00

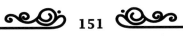

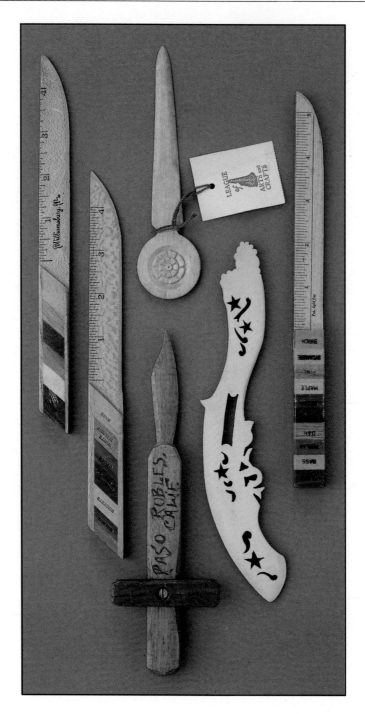

Plate 146. Left to right.

MISCELLANEOUS

Marquetry wood with seven types of wood, also ruler, Williamsburg, Va. $10.00
Marquetry, six labeled woods, ruler, Norfolk, Va. $15.00
Cross, Paso Robles, Calif. $5.00
League of N.H. Arts & Crafts $5.00
Stylized gun with cut outs $5.00
Marquetry with 10 labeled woods & ruler $20.00

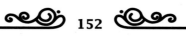

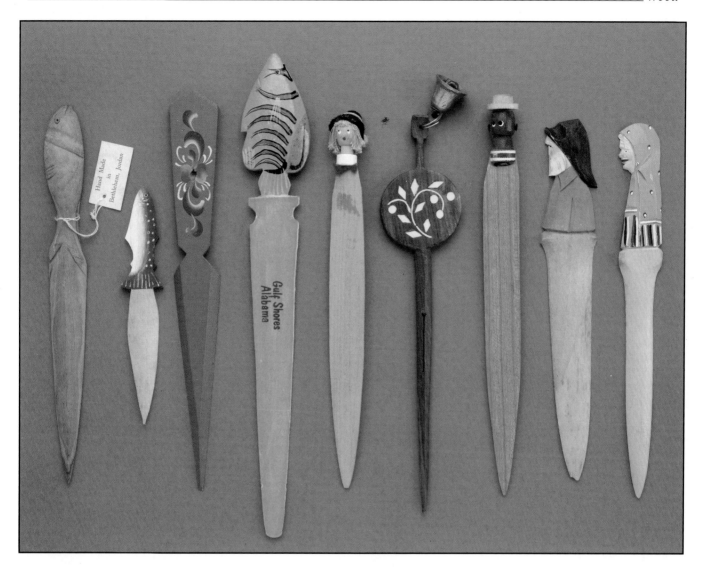

Plate 147. Left to right.

PAINTED

Fish, handmade in Bethlehem, Jordan $8.00
Brown speckled trout, Canada $6.00
Fowle style $5.00
Fish, Gulf Shores, Alabama $8.00
Child's head $8.00
Brass bell with inlay $10.00
Black boy's head $10.00
Old Salt, Canada $10.00
Old lady $10.00

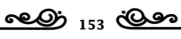

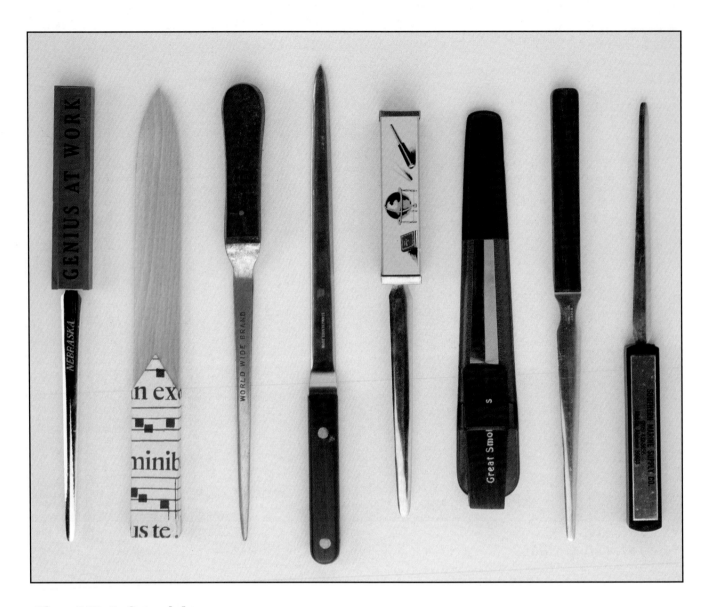

Plate 148. Left to right.

WOOD HANDLES

Genuis at work $3.00
Music motif $3.00
World Wide Brand $4.00
Seattle, Wa. $4.00
Lithographed metal $4.00
Great Smoky Mts., plastic sheath $4.00
West Coast Line $3.00
Southern Marine Supply Co., Mobile, Al. $5.00

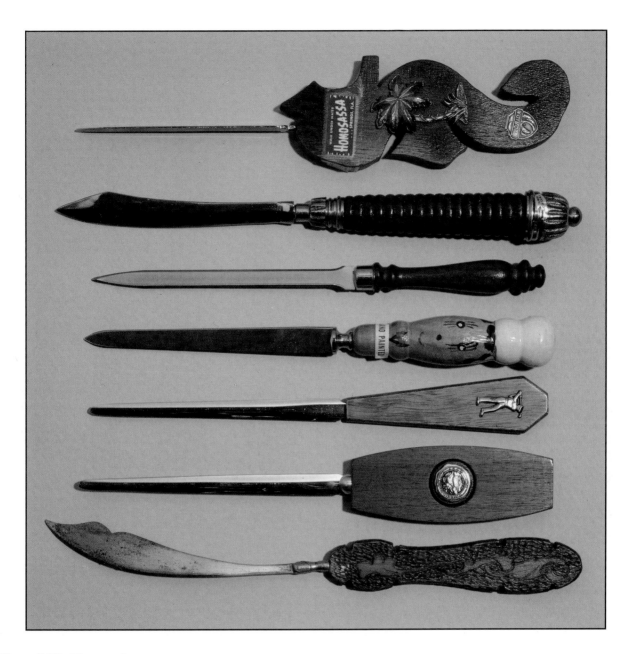

Plate 149. Top to bottom.

WOOD HANDLES

Sea horse with palm tree, Homosassa, Fl. $8.00
Brass fittings, dagger $12.00
Dagger $6.00
Hand-painted chef $10.00
Golfer $10.00
University of Alaska $6.00
Lizard handled dagger $12.00

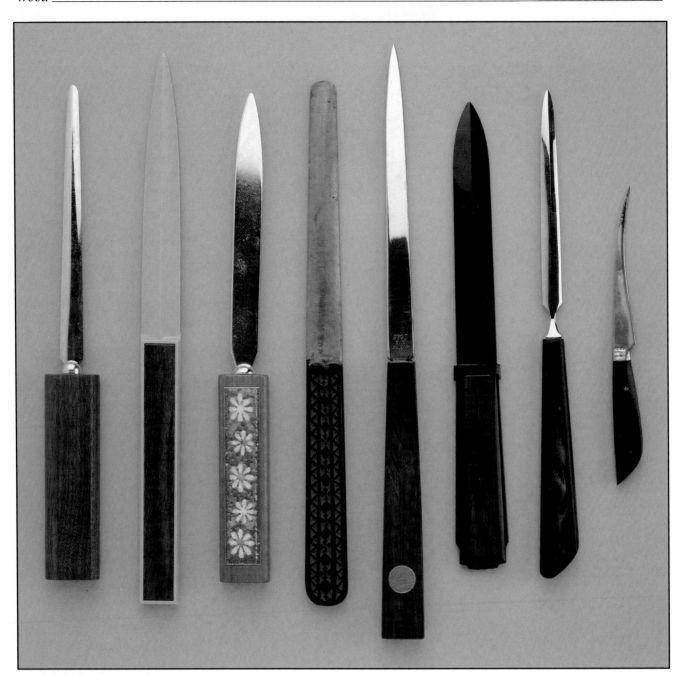

Plate 150. Left to right.

WOOD HANDLES

Plain	$4.00
Plain	$3.00
Floral	$4.00
Carved & painted, Yugoslovia	$6.00
Silver dot	$4.00
Plain	$3.00
Inlaid silver	$10.00
Small brass dagger	$5.00

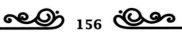

Plate 151. Left to right.

WOOD HANDLES

Fish, Thousand Islands, N.Y. $12.00
Hippo with letter holder mouth $15.00
Native, souvenir of Miami Beach $10.00
Crocodile $12.00
Native god, Panama City, Florida $10.00

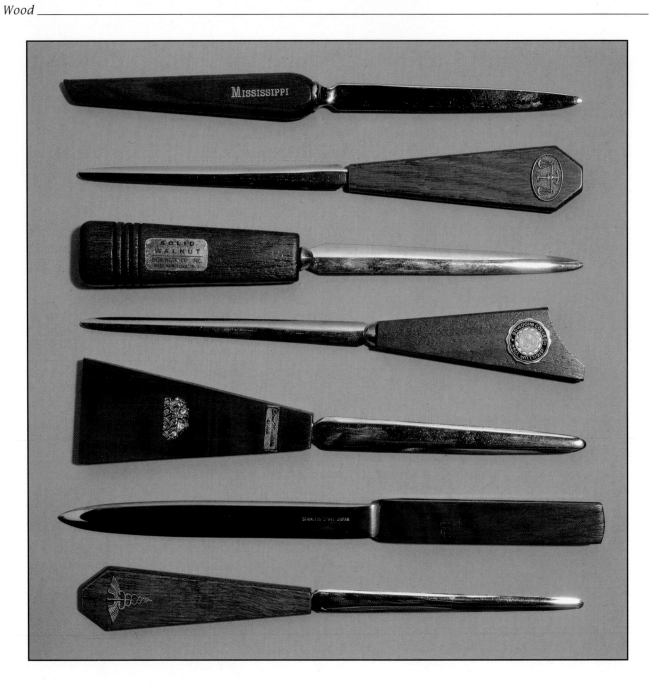

Plate 152. Top to bottom.

Wood Handles

Mississippi $5.00
Libra $5.00
Plain $5.00
Bowdoin College $5.00
Stone Mountain, Ga. $5.00
Plain $4.00
Cadusus $6.00

Bibliography

Flayderman, E. Norman. *Schrimshaw and Scrimshaders.* New Milford., Conn.: N. Flayderman, 1972.

Hansford, S. Howard. *Chinese Carved Jades.* Greenwich, Conn.: NY Graphic Society, 1968.

Ritchie, Carson I. *Bone and Horn Carving.* South Brunswick: A. S. Barnes, 1975.

Schwartz, Jeri. *The Official Identification and Price Guide to Silver and Silverplate.* 6th Ed. House of Collectibles, 1989.

Kovels Antiques and Collectible Price List 1996. NY: Crown Trade Paperbacks, 1996.

Kehr, Ernest A. *The Romance of Stamp. Collecting.* NY: Thomas Y. Crowell Co., 2nd Printing 1948.

The Postal Service Guide to U. S. Stamps, 16th Ed. 1990 Stamp Values, Crawfordsville, IN: U. S. Postal Service Publishing, Printed by R. R. Donnelley and Sons Co.,

The 1991 Scott Standart Postage Stamp Catalogue, Vol. I, 147th Edition. Sidney, Ohio: Scott Publishing Co., 1990.

Huges, Elizabeth and Lester, Marion. *The Big Book of Buttons,* 2nd Printing. Sedgwick ME: New Leaf, 1991.

Funk & Wagnalls New Encyclopedia. USA: Funk & Wagnalls Inc.,1983.

Schroeder's ANTIQUES Price Guide

. . . is the #1 best-selling antiques & collectibles value guide on the market today, and here's why . . .

Identification & Values Of Over 50,000 Antiques & Collectibles

8½ x 11, 608 Pages, $12.95

• *More than 300 advisors, well-known dealers, and top-notch collectors work together with our editors to bring you accurate information regarding pricing and identification.*

• *More than 45,000 items in almost 500 categories are listed along with hundreds of sharp original photos that illustrate not only the rare and unusual, but the common, popular collectibles as well.*

• *Each large close-up shot shows important details clearly. Every subject is represented with histories and background information, a feature not found in any of our competitors' publications.*

• *Our editors keep abreast of newly developing trends, often adding several new categories a year as the need arises.*

If it merits the interest of today's collector, you'll find it in *Schroeder's*. And you can feel confident that the information we publish is up to date and accurate. Our advisors thoroughly check each category to spot inconsistencies, listings that may not be entirely reflective of market dealings, and lines too vague to be of merit. Only the best of the lot remains for publication.

Without doubt, you'll find
SCHROEDER'S ANTIQUES PRICE GUIDE
the only one to buy for
reliable information and values.

COLLECTOR BOOKS
A Division of Schroeder Publishing Co., Inc.